Cambridge Elements ≡

Elements in Corpus Linguistics
edited by
Susan Hunston
University of Birmingham

MULTIMODAL NEWS ANALYSIS ACROSS CULTURES

Helen Caple
University of New South Wales

Changpeng Huan
Shanghai Jiao Tong University

Monika Bednarek
The University of Sydney

CAMBRIDGE
UNIVERSITY PRESS

CAMBRIDGE
UNIVERSITY PRESS

University Printing House, Cambridge CB2 8BS, United Kingdom

One Liberty Plaza, 20th Floor, New York, NY 10006, USA

477 Williamstown Road, Port Melbourne, VIC 3207, Australia

314–321, 3rd Floor, Plot 3, Splendor Forum, Jasola District Centre,
New Delhi – 110025, India

79 Anson Road, #06–04/06, Singapore 079906

Cambridge University Press is part of the University of Cambridge.

It furthers the University's mission by disseminating knowledge in the pursuit of
education, learning, and research at the highest international levels of excellence.

www.cambridge.org
Information on this title: www.cambridge.org/9781108814072
DOI: 10.1017/9781108886048

© Helen Caple, Changpeng Huan and Monika Bednarek 2020

First published 2020

A catalogue record for this publication is available from the British Library.

ISBN 978-1-108-81407-2 Paperback
ISSN 2632-8097 (online)
ISSN 2632-8089 (print)

Additional resources for this publication at www.cambridge.org/9781108814072.

Multimodal News Analysis across Cultures

Elements in Corpus Linguistics

DOI: 10.1017/9781108886048
First published online: September 2020

Helen Caple
University of New South Wales

Changpeng Huan
Shanghai Jiao Tong University

Monika Bednarek
The University of Sydney

Author for correspondence: Helen Caple, helen.caple@unsw.edu.au

Abstract: Corpus-based discourse analysts are becoming increasingly interested in the incorporation of non-linguistic data, for example through corpus-assisted multimodal discourse analysis. This Element applies this new approach in relation to how *news values* are discursively constructed through language and photographs. Using case studies of news from China and Australia, the Element presents a cross-linguistic comparison of news values in national day reporting. Discursive news values analysis (DNVA) has so far been mainly applied to English-language data. This Element offers a new investigation of Chinese DNVA and provides momentum to scholars around the world who are already adopting DNVA to their local contexts. With its focus on national days across two very different cultures, the Element also contributes to research on national identity and cross-linguistic corpus linguistics.

Keywords: Australia Day, China National Day, corpus-assisted multimodal discourse analysis, cross-linguistic analysis, discursive news values analysis, national day, national identity, newsworthiness, news values

ISBNs: 9781108814072 (PB), 9781108886048 (OC)
ISSNs: 2632-8097 (online), 2632-8089 (print)

Contents

1 Corpus-Assisted Multimodal Discourse Analysis and the Newsworthiness of National Day Reporting

1.1 Introduction

Corpus-based discourse analysts are becoming increasingly interested in the incorporation of non-linguistic data, for example, through corpus-assisted multi-modal discourse analysis, or 'CAMDA' (Bednarek & Caple, 2014: 151). CAMDA is concerned with combining corpus linguistic techniques for language analysis with discourse analysis of other semiotic modes. This is especially relevant for corpus data that are inherently multimodal, such as news items, which often contain photographs. If corpus-based discourse analysis of such multimodal texts is limited to analysis of language, this analysis may not provide a full picture of the meanings made in these texts (Caple, 2018a). This Element therefore uses CAMDA to study news texts, examining both news language and news photography. Another area of current interest in corpus-assisted discourse studies consists of attempts to move beyond analysis of a single language (most often, English) to use corpus techniques in cross-linguistic studies (see further Section 1.3.2). In this Element, we therefore use CAMDA to study both Chinese and English news texts.

The particular lens through which we approach our data is that of *news values* – a concept that originates from outside linguistics (see Caple, 2018b) but that has more recently started to play a bigger role in the linguistic analysis of the news media. Using case studies of news from China and Australia, this Element thus presents a cross-linguistic comparison of news values and newsworthiness in national day reporting. Newsworthiness concerns the worth of an event to be reported as news, as constructed via a set of established news values (such as Negativity, Proximity, Eliteness, Unexpectedness, etc.). We examine how these *news values* are discursively constructed through language and photography in our datasets. A new framework, discursive news values analysis (DNVA), has recently been developed to systematically examine how news values are con-structed through such semiotic resources. However, a comprehensive analysis of news values necessitates close discourse analysis of full texts, which is not always possible. The question, then, is, how can corpus linguistic analysis contribute to discursive news values analysis? This Element therefore also illustrates how a non-linguistic concept, such as news values, can be approached from a linguistic perspective, and how we might apply corpus linguistic techniques in its analysis. It also takes up the call to apply and test DNVA on news stories published in different languages and in different cultural contexts (Bednarek & Caple, 2017: 237). In order to keep other variables under control, we have chosen to investigate a similar event across two countries: the 'National Day' of China, celebrated annually on 1 October, and the 'National Day' of Australia, celebrated annually on 26 January.

The National Day of the People's Republic of China is a public holiday celebrating the national day. It is described as a day of patriotism and national celebration and includes government-organised fireworks displays, concerts and sporting and cultural events; public spaces are decorated in festive themes and portraits of revered leaders, such as Mao Zedong, are displayed in public squares (Public Holidays Global, 2019). Important ceremonial features of the national day commemorations include the laying of wreaths at the Monument to the People's Heroes in Tian'anmen Square and national flag raising ceremonies that take place all over the country. While the national day falls on 1 October, the whole week is given over to its celebration, with workers receiving paid holidays and the opportunity to make long-distance family visits. The week is known as the Golden Week (黄金周/ *huangjinzhou*). In every fifth and tenth year, the celebrations are much larger and include military parades, and the national day in 2019 saw the celebration of seventy years of the foundation of the People's Republic of China. However, we deliberately focused on two ordinary years: 2015 and 2016.

The national day public holiday in Australia is officially known as Australia Day. The Australia Day Council (2018) defines it as a 'day to reflect on what it means to be Australian, to celebrate contemporary Australia and to acknowledge our history'. However, the date – 26 January – chosen to celebrate the national day falls on a very controversial date in the history of this nation. This is the date, in 1788, that the First Fleet of British ships landed on the shores of the country now known as Australia. To many Aboriginal and Torres Strait Islander people it marks the invasion of their lands and the beginnings of the oppression of First Nations peoples, and many therefore regard it 'as a day of sorrow and mourning' (Australia Day Council, 2018). Indeed, a 'Day of Mourning' was first proclaimed by Aboriginal activists on 26 January 1938, coinciding with the 150th anniversary of the British arrival (AIATSIS, 2018). Recent years have seen an increase in discussion about how to acknowledge this history, including a 'change the date' campaign.[1] As a result of such activism, there are a number of alternative labels in use for the national day, including *Invasion Day* and *Survival Day*. Eades (2006: 154) uses the term *lexical*

---

[1] There is a diversity of views and opinions towards the national day and the campaign to change the date in Australia. For example, some want the date changed, some want it to remain the same, some call for a new national holiday, some may even be unaware of the debate. Those who do not want the date changed may have different reasons, including that changing the date is meaningless without changing the nation (Trindall 2019). For a few different answers from Aboriginal and Torres Strait Islander people to the question 'What do you do on 26 January?', see University of Sydney (2018).

struggle to refer to the 'struggle over labels, descriptions, or lexical items' in the legal system (i.e. how events, issues, acts etc. are referred to). But such lexical struggles can also be observed in society at large, as in the case of the different labels for the Australian national day. Such a lexical struggle is also indicative of a *discursive struggle* in society (i.e. a struggle between discourses that compete with each other to define aspects of the social world).[2] This makes Australia a particularly interesting site for a case study.

Why did we decide to focus on the reporting of national days? First, national days are interesting because they differ from most other news events in that they recur on a yearly basis and are covered by newspapers each year (ben-Aaron, 2003). Second, most countries have national days, which enables cross-cultural comparison. Third, national days are closely tied to the history of a nation and the discursive construction of national identity. As ben-Aaron (2003: 77) notes, national holidays are a manifestation of 'applied nationalism', and their coverage by newspapers may 'have a political subtext, such as mobilising for war, promoting a policy or platform, or reconstituting the nation in minority inclusive or exclusive terms'. Such public holidays are therefore important in relation to what Anderson (1991) calls the 'imagining' of nations. On the one hand, the celebration of national days itself is aimed at producing national community and cohesion. On the other hand, media discourse about national days is also important for the discursive construction of national identity, unity and the promotion of patriotism (Ting, 2017). It comes as no surprise that news reporting about the national day in the United States (Independence Day) respects both the positive and the negative face of the nation, by 'praising it, identifying with it ... and acting in its interests' and by 'avoiding conflict with it' (ben-Aaron, 2003: 98). Historically, such holiday news falls on the 'expected, consonant, positive side of the news value scales' (ben-Aaron, 2003: 98–9). In other words, we might assume that the news value of Negativity plays little or no role in such coverage. In the Chinese data, we hypothesise that this will be even more true given the role of media censorship and the importance of

---

[2] The notion of *discursive struggle* is often linked to Laclau and Mouffe's (1985) discourse theory (e.g. Jørgensen & Phillips, 2002, Carpentier, 2018). In this theory,

> [d]ifferent discourses – each of them representing particular ways of talking about and understanding the social world – are engaged in a constant struggle with one other to achieve hegemony, that is, to fix the meanings of language in their own way. Hegemony, then, can provisionally be understood as the dominance of one particular perspective. (Jørgensen & Phillips, 2002: 6–7)

However, the term *discursive struggle* is in general widely used in discourse studies. The earliest use in English that we have been able to identify comes from Belsey (1984: 29), who uses the term *discursive struggle* in a paper that draws on Foucault, Derrida, and Marx to emphasise the politics and plurality of meaning.

Positivity (see Section 1.2.2). Since it is commonly assumed that the news media maintain dominant or hegemonic perspectives and that government and other elites are much more visible than minorities, we would also expect such positive reporting in the Australian news media. In both countries, we would furthermore expect that the reporting of national days is used as an opportunity for the promotion of national unity and cohesion. At the same time, because of the differences in Chinese and Australian news media landscapes, political systems, historical contexts and cultural attitudes towards national identity and nationalism, we also expect to see differences, which are perhaps less easy to predict.[3] Our respective analyses are presented in Sections 2 and 3 of this Element. In this introductory section we first present an overview of the concept of news values, including discursive news values analysis, and then describe our data and approach – cross-linguistic CAMDA.

1.2 News Values

As mentioned, the concept of news values originates from outside linguistics. It has been widely drawn upon in journalism studies, where it has also been hotly debated. With some exceptions (e.g. Bell, 1991, Bednarek, 2006, Cotter, 2010), the concept has not figured prominently in linguistics, although this is now changing. Bednarek and Caple (2017) review news values at length and we do not want to repeat this here. Rather, we will use this section to introduce our own approach to news values. Readers interested in the justifications for this approach and how it differs from others are advised to consult this earlier work.

It is important to emphasise that we restrict the term *news values* to 'news-worthiness values' that relate to reported news events or news actors. We exclude other aspects such as moral–ethical values (e.g. truth, impartiality, honesty), commercial values (e.g. speed, access via multiple platforms), news writing objectives (general news writing goals such as clarity of expression, brevity, etc.), and other factors that play important roles in the news process (e.g. content mix, space constraints, the availability of a reporter, material or sources, audience analytics, news cycles, etc.). Additionally, when we talk about an event's potential news value, we mean a value that is socioculturally assigned, rather than 'natural' or 'inherent' in the event. We use the term *event* as a cover term for both semiotic and material events, that is, issues and happenings, including elements or aspects

---

[3] We further acknowledge that contestation of 'National Days' can stem from the very nature of the event being commemorated: National Days can be Independence Days (e.g. USA, Singapore), or Foundation Days (e.g. China, France), or "Discovery" Days (e.g. Australia). Therefore, the difference between the Chinese and the Australian reporting is not just a matter of national culture, but a difference in the nature of what is being celebrated.

of these. For example, when we talk about how events are constructed as newsworthy, this includes the event's news actors or its location.

1.2.1 Definition

Our approach to news values recognises that there are different dimensions to news values. This means that newsworthiness can be approached from various perspectives: an event in its material reality holds potential news value for a given community (material perspective); news workers and audience members have beliefs about news values and newsworthiness (cognitive perspective); news values are applied as selection criteria in journalistic practice (social perspective); and news values can be communicated through discourse (discursive perspective). As discourse analysts, it is the discursive perspective that we are adopting here. More specifically, we align ourselves with the perspective on discourse as language in use and consider *discourse* as multimodal. This means we are interested in analysing how news values are constructed through semiotic resources, that is, in the linguistic devices and visual techniques that are used in multimodal news stories to establish the 'newsworthiness' of reported events.

In contrast to most other approaches to news values, this perspective does not treat news values as pre- and therefore a-textual. The question is not how an event is selected as news (selection), but how it is constructed as news (presentation/treatment). We analyse how specific events are constructed as newsworthy in published news stories. Importantly, this discourse analysis is not meant to tell us anything about speaker intentionality or audience effects, but rather focuses on the meaning potential of texts. We do nevertheless make a general assumption about news discourse, namely that it 'is intended to attract an audience through presenting a story to them that is newsworthy' (Bednarek & Caple, 2012: 46).

Our aim is not to reduce values to discourse or to assume that they are only constructed through discourse. We simply argue that the study of news values should incorporate a more systematic analysis of how they are established in discourse. We use verbs such as *establish, construct* or *construe* in order to underline that texts have a constitutive dimension in what Fairclough (1995) regards as the dialectical relationship between texts and culture. In his words, '[t]exts are socioculturally shaped but they also constitute society and culture, in ways which may be transformative as well as reproductive' (Fairclough, 1995: 34). There is a 'top-down' aspect of social reproduction, but there is also a 'bottom-up' aspect of social reproduction, where social practices sustain, continue and change the system (van Dijk, 1998: 229). Importantly, top-down aspects do matter and events in their material reality put constraints on how they can be discursively constructed. Our choice of verbs such as *construct/construe/ establish* simply highlights the power of discourse and represents a much-needed shift in emphasis in news values research.

In sum, we systematically link commonly recognised news values (such as Eliteness, Impact, Negativity, Proximity, etc.) to the verbal and visual semiotic resources that have the potential to establish these values in published news stories. This provides a framework for analysis, in that we can identify forms, expressions and techniques that establish newsworthiness in such texts. The specific verbal and visual semiotic resources that provide the framework for discourse analysis – whether corpus-assisted or 'manual', whether monomodal or multimodal – are described in more detail in the next section.

1.2.2 News Values and Semiotic Resources

There are ongoing debates around the number and types of news values and the labels used to refer to them. Based on a basic consensus around commonly recognised news values and considering the advantages/disadvantages of particular labels, we work with a list of eleven news values (see Table 1.1).

Table 1.1 The news values and their definitions

News value	Definition
Aesthetic Appeal	The event is discursively constructed as beautiful (visuals only)
Consonance	The event is discursively constructed as (stereo)typical (limited here to news actors, social groups, organisations, or countries/nations)[a]
Eliteness	The event is discursively constructed as of high status or fame (including but not limited to the people, countries or institutions involved)
Impact	The event is discursively constructed as having significant effects or consequences (not necessarily limited to impact on the target audience)
Negativity	The event is discursively constructed as negative, for example as a disaster, conflict, controversy, criminal act
Personalisation	The event is discursively constructed as having a personal or 'human' face (involving non-elite actors, including eyewitnesses)

Table 1.1 (cont.)

News value	Definition
Positivity	The event is discursively constructed as positive, for example as a scientific breakthrough or heroic act
Proximity	The event is discursively constructed as geographically or culturally near (in relation to the publication location/ target audience)
Superlativeness	The event is discursively constructed as being of high intensity or large scope/scale
Timeliness	The event is discursively constructed as timely in relation to the publication date: as new, recent, ongoing, about to happen or otherwise relevant to the immediate situation/time (current or seasonal)
Unexpectedness	The event is discursively constructed as unexpected, for example as unusual, strange, rare

[a] Consonance is defined as the construction of an event's news actors, social groups, organisations or countries/nations in a way that conforms to stereotypes that members of the target audience hold about them.

Importantly, Aesthetic Appeal only applies to visuals, while Positivity is a news value that does not apply to all types of news stories. It is useful, however, to be able to consider both Negativity and Positivity in order to explore whether a particular event/topic is constructed as more negative or positive. We must emphasise that Positivity does not equate to positive evaluation, nor does Negativity equate to negative evaluation. For instance, references to clashes between protestors and police construct Negativity, as they point to conflict, regardless of whether the newspaper 'sides with' the protestors or the police (Bednarek & Caple, 2017: 61). Further elaboration on these and other issues as well as extensive explanations of each news value can be found in Bednarek and Caple (2017).

Since the news values are deliberately broad, researchers can dig deeper in their analysis, if required. For example, in relation to Eliteness we could distinguish between references to celebrities, politicians, athletes, academics, officials, etc. In relation to Negativity, we could analyse what type of Negativity is established (e.g. accidents vs. opposition/division vs. terrorism vs. crime). This is an approach that we will adopt in this Element, where appropriate. News values are also scalar – for instance, references to police chiefs construct a higher degree of Eliteness than references to ordinary police officers ('weak'

Eliteness), and references to locations in the same city as the target audience construct a higher degree of Proximity than references to the whole country of the target audience. However, it is difficult to objectively quantify the extent to which a linguistic resource constructs a particular news value, for example by applying a numerical weight to it. For this reason, we adopt a categorial approach in this Element, although we occasionally comment on this where particularly relevant.

Bell (1991: 155) suggests that these news values are valid for many countries, and this seems to be the case for China. Through newsroom observations at a Chinese news organisation, Huan (2018) found that similar news values are part of daily editorial discussions. Specifically, daily editorial meetings tended to foreground Personalisation, with events also discussed in term of Eliteness, Impact, Timeliness, and Proximity. Analysing Chinese news reporting of risk events, Huan (2016, 2018) found a clear co-patterning of Eliteness and Positivity in relation to elites, while constructions of Personalisation and Negativity related to ordinary citizens. Historically, the Chinese news media have had a reputation of reporting only positive news (Shi-xu, 2014: 86), maintaining the 'normative Chinese value of harmony' (Wu & Ng, 2011: 80). However, in relation to broadcast and international news, Wu and Ng (2011) report an increase in negative news. Shi-xu (2014: 86) also notes that more attention is now being paid to 'bad news', including in key Communist Party outlets such as *People's Daily*. However, further empirical studies are needed to capture more recent shifts in news values in the Chinese news media.

Bell (1991: 65) made the important observation that news values can be 'enhanced' through language by journalists, and that 'maximizing news value is the primary function' (Bell, 1991: 76) of copy editing, illustrating this with authentic examples. This provided us with an important impetus for the development of our own 'discursive' approach – namely the idea that news discourse can be systematically examined for its construction of newsworthiness. We have taken this further and have developed comprehensive inventories for the semiotic resources that have the potential to construct these eleven news values. We provide a summary of our framework here, with selected examples used for illustration (see Table 1.2). A more detailed explanation is provided in Bednarek and Caple (2017). Researchers interested in undertaking DNVA themselves should not rely on the brief introduction here, but rather consult this earlier book-length treatment and other relevant literature listed at www.newsvaluesanalysis.com.

Table 1.2 Linguistic and visual resources that have the potential to construct news values

News value	The event is constructed as . . .	Linguistic resources	Visual resources
Aesthetic Appeal	aesthetically pleasing	N/A [this news value only applies to visual resources; see Bednarek & Caple 2017: 66–7]	**Represented participants:** • The depiction of people, places, objects, landscapes culturally recognised for their beauty. **Composition: Balance** • Dynamic, asymmetric composition, making use of diagonal axis; • Balanced, symmetrical photos where the symmetry is momentarily interrupted. **Technical affordances:** • Movement: blurring and freezing of action; • Noise: high level of graininess; • Focus: lengthening or reducing depth of field within the photo.

Table 1.2 (cont.)

News value	The event is constructed as …	Linguistic resources	Visual resources
Consonance	(stereo)typical	References to stereotypical attributes or preconceptions; assessments of expectedness/typicality (*typical, famed for*); similarity with past (*yet another, once again*); explicit references to general knowledge/ traditions, etc. (*well-known*)	**Represented participants/Attributes:** • The depiction of people and their attributes that fit with the stereotypical imagery of a person/country etc. (e.g. beer and breasts for Germany's Oktoberfest). **Activity sequence:** • Staged/highly choreographed depictions of typical activities associated with a person/ group/nation.
Eliteness	of high status or fame (including news actors, organisations, etc.)	Various status markers, including role labels (*Professor Roger Stone, experts*); status-indicating adjectives (*the prestigious Man Booker prize, top diplomats*); recognised names (*Donald Trump*); descriptions of achievement/fame (*were selling millions of records a year*); use by	**Represented participants:** • Showing known and easily recognisable key figures, e.g. political leaders, celebrities. **Attributes:** • Showing people in elaborate costumes, uniform or with other regalia of officialdom; • Showing self-reflexive elements like microphones/cameras.

	news actors/sources of specialised/technical terminology, high-status accent or sociolect [especially in broadcast news]	**Activity sequence:** • Showing people flanked by military, police or bodyguards or in a media scrum; • Showing people using the specialist equipment associated with elite professions (e.g. surgeon performing an operation). **Setting:** • Showing context associated with an elite profession, e.g. books, lab, police station. **Represented participants/attributes:** • Showing the after-effects (often negative) of events, e.g. scenes of destruction, injuries, damage to property; • Showing emotions caused by an event.
Impact	having significant effects or consequences (not limited to impact on the target audience)	Assessments of significance (*momentous, historic, crucial*); representation of actual or non-actual significant/relevant consequences, including abstract, material or mental effects (*note that will stun the world, Australia could be left with no policy, leaving scenes of destruction*)	
Negativity	negative	References to negative emotion and attitude (*distraught, condemn*); negative evaluative language (*terrible*); negative lexis (*conflict, damage, death*); descriptions of negative (e.g. norm-breaking) behaviour (*has broken his promise*)	**Represented participants/attributes:** • Showing negative events and their effects, e.g. the aftermath of accidents, natural disasters, the injured/wounded, the wreckage/damage done to property; • Showing people experiencing negative emotions.

Table 1.2 (cont.)

News value	The event is constructed as . . .	Linguistic resources	Visual resources
			Activity sequence: • Showing people being arrested or (as defendant) with lawyers/barristers/police; • Showing people attempting to hide their identity, e.g. using an item of clothing to cover the head, or showing aggression towards the camera, e.g. putting a hand up in front of the lens; • Showing people engaging in norm-breaking behaviour, e.g. fighting, vandalising, stealing, attacking. **Technical affordances:** • Movement/blurring involving negative content (resulting in poor quality photos); • Noise: dramatising and intensifying negative content; • Focus: where extreme circumstances mean inability to provide sharp and detailed image content, e.g. water/rain on the lens;

Personalisation[a]	having a personal or 'human' face (involving non-elite actors)	References to 'ordinary' people, their emotions, experiences (*Charissa Benjamin and her Serbian husband*, *'It was pretty bloody scary'*, *But one of his victims sobbed, Deborah said afterwards: 'My sentence has only just begun'*); use by news actors/ sources of 'everyday' spoken language, accent, sociolect [especially in broadcast news]	• In moving images: blurring and movement caused by camera-people moving around, running, ducking to avoid projectiles etc. (suggesting unstable situation, i.e. danger). **Represented participants/attributes:** • Showing 'ordinary' individuals, especially when singled out and standing in for a larger group; • People dressed in informal/everyday clothing; • Carrying items such as rucksacks, handbags, shopping bags; • Showing an emotional response. **Setting:** • In the home/domestic setting; • On the street. **Composition: Salience** • Positioning individuals in unequal relation (in terms of textual composition, **not** in terms of social power dynamics) to others in the image frame, e.g. singling out one individual through foregrounding or backgrounding.

Table 1.2 (cont.)

News value	The event is constructed as …	Linguistic resources	Visual resources
			Composition: Shot length • Using a close-up shot (to focus on a person's emotion, for example). **Technical affordances: Focus** • Reducing depth of field so that the focus remains on the individual.
Positivity	positive	References to positive emotion and attitude (*joy, celebrate*); positive evaluative language (*brilliant*); positive lexis (*success, win, help*); descriptions of positive behaviour (*unveiled a cabinet with an equal number of men and women*)	**Represented participants/attributes:** • Showing people experiencing positive emotions. **Activity sequence:** • Showing people engaging in positively valued behaviour, e.g. being successful at red carpet events, award ceremonies; • Showing actions associated with reconciliation or praise, e.g. shaking hands, hugging.
Proximity	geographically or culturally near (the target audience)	Explicit references to place or nationality near the target community (*Australia, Canberra woman*);	**Represented participants/Attributes/Setting:** • Showing well-known or iconic landmarks (Tower Bridge, Sydney Opera House, Golden

| Superlativeness | of high intensity or large scope | references to the nation/community via deictics, generic place references, adjectives (*here, the nation's capital, home-grown*); inclusive first person plural pronouns (*our nation's leaders*); use by news actors/sources of [geographical] accent/dialect [especially in broadcast news]; cultural references (*haka, prom*)

Intensifiers (*severe, dramatically*); quantifiers (*thousands, huge*); intensified lexis (*panic, smash*); metaphor and simile (*a tsunami of crime, like a World War II battle*); comparison (*the largest drug ring in Detroit history*); repetition (*building after building flattened*); lexis of growth (*a growing list of, scaling up efforts*); only/just/alone/already + time/distance or related lexis (*only hours after*) | Gate Bridge, the Shard), natural features (Uluru) or cultural symbols (flags, national colours/distinctive uniforms).

[Verbal text:
• Showing verbal text indicating relevant place/cultural connection, e.g. signage.]

Represented participants:
• Showing the large-scale repetition of participants in the image frame, e.g. not just one house but an entire street affected;
• Showing **extreme** (positive or negative) emotions in participants.

Composition: Shot length
• Use of very wide angle to exaggerate differences in size/space;
• Magnification (larger-than-life representation) through use of extreme close-up or macro lens. |

Table 1.2 (cont.)

News value	The event is constructed as …	Linguistic resources	Visual resources
			Technical affordances: Movement • Camera movement and blurring, combined with camera-people moving around, running, ducking to avoid projectiles etc. (suggesting seriousness/high danger, etc.).
Timeliness	timely in relation to the publication date: new, recent, ongoing, about to happen, current or seasonal	Temporal references (*today, yesterday's, within days, now*); present and present perfect (*it is testing our emergency resources*); implicit time references through lexis (*continues, ongoing, have begun to*); reference to current trends, seasonality, change/newness (*its 'word of the year' for 2015, keep their homes well heated this winter, after fresh revelations, for the first time, a new role as*)	**Represented participants:** • Natural phenomena that indicate time, e.g. the season may be implied in the depiction of flora or environmental conditions; • Inclusion of cultural artefacts, such as Christmas trees, which are representative of a particular time of year. **Activity sequence:** • Showing the revealing of an item, to be seen for the first time. **[Verbal Text:** • Including verbal text indicating relevant time, e.g. signage.]

| Unexpectedness | unexpected | Evaluations of unexpectedness (*different, astonishing, strange*), references to surprise/expectations (*shock at North Cottesloe quiz night, people just really can't believe it*); comparisons that indicate unusuality (*the first time since 1958*); references to unusual happenings (*British man survives 15-storey plummet*) | **Represented participants:**
• Showing people being shocked/surprised;
• Showing unusual happenings that would be considered outside an established societal norm or expectation.

Composition: Salience
• Juxtaposition of elements in the frame that create stark contrast. |

[a] Following Bednarek and Caple (2017: 120–1), we do not analyse all photographs depicting humans as constructing Personalisation. Personalisation concerns the singling out of ordinary people from larger groups who they may also come to represent. Personalisation is constructed through the emotional responses of ordinary individuals, through compositional choices of shot type (close, personal) and positioning within the image frame (in a more salient position compared to others). Photographs of large groups, and where participants have their backs to the camera or are unidentifiable do not construct Personalisation

Importantly, there is no one-to-one relationship between language and news value. On the one hand, the same linguistic device can be used to construe different news values. Thus, quasi-titles can either construct Eliteness (*Top scientist Christoph Gabor*) or Personalisation (*Mother-of-two Ms Adkins*). On the other hand, the same linguistic device can simultaneously construct several news values, as when negative intensified lexis represents an event's effects (*town **ravaged** by bushfires*), thus construing both Negativity and Impact. In addition, there is no closed list of resources – news values can be constructed by an open-ended range of lexical or grammatical resources (word forms, lemmas, phrases, whole clauses or sentences). Although we can include some typical examples in our inventory, we are not able to list **all** possible devices.

Finally, the inventory of resources in Table 1.2 should not be mechanically and unreflectively applied. It is not appropriate, for example, to count every single time reference as constructing Timeliness or every place reference as constructing Proximity. Language is multifunctional and words vary their meaning according to co-text and context. News values are also context-dependent. The same linguistic resources can, for example, construct Proximity or Eliteness for one readership, but not for another. We need to take into account the target audience of the news outlet and the time and location of the publication, and we need to carefully consider the likely meaning potential of each resource as used in the text. For example, does it construct the event as negative, unexpected, recent, near? This is not an exact science and there will be different interpretations of texts. It is good practice to analyse news values in publications where the analyst has a high familiarity with the target audience. Thus, as Australian and Chinese researchers, we analyse news stories published in Australian and Chinese news outlets.

To consolidate and clarify the discussion thus far, we offer a brief example of DNVA. Figure 1.1 presents a short extract of the beginning of a story published by *The Sydney Morning Herald*, Australia, on 21 October 2019.[4]

In the verbal text, Negativity is constructed through negative lexis (e.g. *defy ban*; *set fire to*; *turned violent*), including lexis pointing specifically to conflict (e.g. *protesters*; *rally against*). Superlativeness is constructed through emphasising the number of people involved (e.g. *tens of thousands*; *mass rally*). Eliteness is construed in relation to the target of the protests (*Carrie Lam's government*). Timeliness is established through explicit reference to the recent past (*on Sunday afternoon*, with the story published on Monday morning). Despite the presence of place references (*Hong Kong*; *Kowloon*), Proximity is not constructed here, since the target audience is readers in Sydney, New South Wales in Australia. One of

---

[4] The full story can be viewed at www.smh.com.au/world/asia/tens-of-thousands-defy-ban-to-protest-in-hong-kong-tourist-district-20191020-p532hf.html (accessed 21 October 2019).

Tens of thousands defy
ban to protest

Kirsty Needham   Monday 21 Oct 2019 6:00 am

Protesters return tear gas canisters to riot police during a rally in Hong Kong. **AP**

Hong Kong: Protesters set fire to train station entrances and threw petrol bombs at two police stations as a mass rally in Kowloon against Carrie Lam's government turned violent on Sunday afternoon.

Figure 1.1 Headline, lead photo and lead paragraph of a hard news story published in smh.com.au, 21 October 2019 (tablet view)

these news values, Negativity, is reinforced in the visual text: The photograph construes Negativity through the depiction of masked protestors hurling gas canisters through the air. Thus, the happening in Hong Kong is multimodally established as newsworthy for the Australian target audience as a serious, recent, negative (conflict-rich) event directed at political authorities.

As this brief analysis illustrates, '[e]xamining how events are endowed with newsworthiness by the news media shows which aspects of the event are emphasised, and reveals the shape in which events are packaged for news consumption by audiences' (Bednarek, 2016a: 31). DNVA can thus be used to analyse the packaging of news **as** news, including the role that different (verbal/ visual) components play in multimodal news stories. Moreover, the analysis of news values can be an additional tool for Critical Discourse Analysis (Bednarek & Caple, 2014), since many researchers have argued that news values are themselves an ideological system. DNVA can also identify the semiotic resources that are repeatedly employed to establish particular news values, i.e. the rhetoric of newsworthiness. Finally, we can analyse if particular topics, events, issues or people are associated with specific news values: our focus in this Element is on news values in the reporting of national days in Chinese and Australian news media.

1.3 Data and Approach

Chinese and Australian newspapers sit at opposite ends of the spectrum in terms of ownership and state control. In China, despite commercialisation of the media,[5] almost all newspapers remain under the control of the Chinese Communist Party (CCP) and/or the government (Shirk, 2011: 9; Sun, 2012: 12; Chan, 2019: 66). In fact, the CCP 'will do whatever it takes to make sure that the information reaching the public through the commercial media and the Internet does not inspire people to challenge party rule' (Gang & Bandurski, 2011: 39; Shirk, 2011: 3; Chan, 2019: 66). National, provincial and local newspapers are tightly censored by the CCP Propaganda Department and State Council Information Offices (Shirk, 2011: 21). Newspapers and agencies such as *People's Daily* (人民日报) and *Xinhua News Agency* (新华社) are state-owned. Yet despite the censorship, commercial newspapers, like *Nanfang Metro* (南方都市报), are held to be 'far more informative and reliable' than the official newspapers (Gang & Bandurski, 2011: 39; Shirk, 2011: 22). In fact, the titles published by the Nanfang Daily Media Group, based in Southern China, are seen as the 'agenda-setters of China's popular media and play an increasingly important role in Chinese domestic politics' (Sun, 2012: 12). It has also been argued that Chinese news media now contain more critical coverage of governments and Chinese society than in the past (Shi-xu, 2014: 120).

In Australia, two major privately owned newspaper companies have dominated the media landscape until 2019. News Corp Australia, a subsidiary of Rupert Murdoch's News Corp empire, has monopoly control over metropolitan newspapers in four of Australia's eight state/territory capital cities, and publishes the only truly generalist national newspaper, *The Australian*. Fairfax Media, the oldest family-operated newspaper company in Australia, shared the stage with News Corp until 2019 when it was sold to the media company Nine Entertainment. Fairfax published the longest running and highest circulation newspaper, *The Sydney Morning Herald*.

---

[5] In 2003, most newspapers became business entities, and enterprises were permitted to invest up to 40 per cent in the news media (Shi-xu, 2014: 119–20).

1.3.1 Datasets

In the construction of our comparative datasets (see Table 1.3), we have attempted to investigate publications that are similar in purview, for example, national newspapers that generally align with their respective governments (though obviously not comparable in terms of raw distribution). By including a metropolitan newspaper in both countries, we also aim to explore the connection between local identity and national belonging, as expressed in reporting about the national day.

From the two Chinese newspapers we collected articles that were published one week before and one week after the national day (on 1 October). To do so, we identified news **about** the national day (not merely mentioning the day), and then collected the relevant text from the online *Database of Chinese Key Newspapers* (中国重要报纸数据库). Opinion texts were excluded. Each file includes the headline, potential sub-headlines, and the body text. The metadata (e.g. author, date) were omitted and each text was saved as plain text in UTF-8 encoding. Each file has a unique ID corresponding to a record in a spreadsheet which contains metadata such as date, author, section, etc. The final corpus consists of 188 articles (102,746 words). We will refer to this dataset as the ChinaDay corpus (see Table 1.4).

Photographs used in the Chinese news reporting were copied from the online version of the newspaper, as stored in the online database, and saved as .jpg, using the same unique story ID as the file name. The total number of news photographs is 131 (see Table 1.5).

From the two Australian newspapers we collected articles that were published between 19 January and 1 February in 2016 and 2017, that is, over a two-week span on either side of the national day (on 26 January). We surveyed the print copies of these two newspapers to identify news about the national day, and then collected the relevant verbal text from an online database (Factiva). A more common method in corpus-based discourse analysis is to use a list of seed words to create a corpus (e.g. Baker et al., 2013: 28), but since we also collected photographs, we needed to access print copies. Our approach to corpus design is also more in line with Sinclair's (2005) recommendations to control subject matter in a corpus through the use of external, or non-linguistic criteria, and to select corpus texts without regard for the language they contain. In other words, the selection of texts was not dependent on whether they contain particular words, phrases or structures. However, in so far as we read the texts to identify whether they were about the national day it is impossible to get away from language influencing text selection entirely.

Articles were made available as plain text files in UFT-8 encoding and in WordSmith's unicode encoding. Each file includes the headline, potential

Table 1.3 The newspapers selected for investigation of reporting on the national day

Newspaper Name	Type	Established	Circulation (week days)	Percentage of population reached	Target Audience
People's Daily 人民日报	Country-wide daily; official newspaper of the CCP (party-controlled; not a business entity)	1948	3 million (2015 data from People's Daily online-People.cn)	> 1%	(predominantly) civil servants at different levels of government
Nanfang Metropolis Daily 南方都市报	Largest metropolitan newspaper in the Pearl River Delta area	1997	Daily circulation: 1,845,000	> 1%	Tertiary-educated business owners, middle to upper class, with high socio-economic status, aged 25–44
The Australian	Country-wide daily; sympathetic to right-leaning governments	1964	116,655 (end 2016) (2.4 million readership)	> 1%	Business owners/leaders, management level, middle to upper class, with high socio-economic status
The Sydney Morning Herald	Largest metropolitan newspaper; sympathetic to left-leaning governments	1841	658,000 (end 2016) (5.2 million readership)	3%	Tertiary-educated, middle class, with high socio-economic status

Table 1.4 Number of articles in the ChinaDay corpus

	People's Daily		*Nanfang Metro*	
Date Range	**2015**	**2016**	**2015**	**2016**
24-September	1	0	3	NA
25-September	0	0	2	NA
26- September	3	0	1	0
27- September	1	1	NA	4
28- September	1	1	5	1
29- September	0	3	5	9
30- September	6	5	7	6
1-October	9	6	1	5
2- October	5	9	4	6
3- October	8	5	4	2
4- October	10	3	3	0
5- October	11	4	1	0
6- October	6	3	0	4
7- October	4	5	4	1
TOTAL	**65**	**45**	**40**	**38**

Table 1.5 Photographs collected
in the Chinese dataset

Newspaper	2015	2016
People's Daily	30	31
Nanfang Metro	39	31

sub-headlines, and the body text. Other elements (author by-line, date-line, photo caption, pull-quotes, other labels, e.g. 'exclusive') were omitted. Each file has a unique ID corresponding to a record in a spreadsheet which contains metadata such as date, author, section, etc. Articles include news stories about the national day as well as associated awards (Australia Day Honours, Australian of the Year). Opinion articles were not collected. The final corpus consists of 136 articles (63,350 words); see Table 1.6.[6] Some 67 of these articles appeared in *The Australian*, while 69 articles were

---

[6] WordSmith; tokens in text; hyphens not allowed in words; ' not allowed within word (separates, e.g. *Australia's* into two tokens, *Australia* and *s*). NA = Sunday, incorporated into 'weekend edition', which is published on a Saturday.

Table 1.6 Number of articles in the AusDay corpus

Date Range	The Australian		The Sydney Morning Herald	
	2016	2017	2016	2017
19-January	0	1	0	0
20-January	0	0	0	2
21-January	0	1	2	1
22-January	0	NA	3	NA
23-January	1	0	3	0
24-January	NA	0	NA	1
25-January	1	2	12	1
26-January	18	16	23	8
27-January	8	8	4	3
28-January	3	4	3	1
29-January	2	NA	1	NA
30-January	2	0	1	0
31-January	NA	0	NA	0
01-February	0	0	0	0
TOTAL	**35**	**32**	**52**	**17**

Table 1.7 Photographs collected in the Australia dataset

Newspaper	2016	2017
The Australian	38	43
The Sydney Morning Herald	48	29

published in *The Sydney Morning Herald*. We will refer to this dataset as the AusDay corpus.

Photographs, where used, were scanned, and saved as .jpg, using the same unique story ID as the file name. The total number of news photographs across the two newspapers is 158 (see Table 1.7).

In terms of the 'material' reality, across the two years of data collection, there was a noticeable increase in the amount of political debate in 2017 compared to 2016. Indeed, throughout 2017, a number of local councils announced changes to their 2018 Australia Day celebrations, opting to remove all references to Australia Day, no longer holding public celebrations, and in the case of Yarra

Council in North Melbourne, replacing citizenship ceremonies with an event 'marking the loss of Indigenous culture' (Clure, 2017, Walhquist, 2017). While our analysis treats the corpus as a composite, future research could investigate potential diachronic changes across the years in terms of how they reflect such societal developments.

1.3.2 Approach
Cross-Linguistic Corpus-Assisted Multimodal Research

As mentioned previously, the research presented in this Element is an example of cross-linguistic corpus-assisted multimodal analysis, or cross-linguistic CAMDA (Bednarek & Caple, 2014: 151). It brings together corpus linguistics and discourse analysis, as well as the analysis of different modes (multimodality), and compares data from two different languages. There is a sound tradition of multimodal discourse analysis (e.g. Machin & Mayr, 2012, Caple, 2013, Machin, 2013, Djonov & Zhao, 2014), as well as corpus-based or corpus-assisted discourse analysis (e.g. Mautner, 2000, Baker et al., 2008, Partington et al., 2013, Nartey & Mwinlaaru, 2019). However, most corpus-assisted discourse studies are monolingual, as Vessey (2013) points out, while cross-linguistic studies have only recently started to emerge. This is most likely because such studies face a variety of challenges (Vessey, 2013, Taylor, 2014). Most of the existing research tends to rely on the identification of comparable terms across languages, that is, on items with functional equivalence – either for the purpose of constructing comparable corpora (as seed terms), or for analysis of node words (Taylor, 2014: 373–4). Table 1.8 shows some examples from selected research (for additional studies, see overviews in Vessey, 2013 or Taylor, 2014).

A corpus-driven approach appears to be less frequently used, although Baker and Vessey (2018) start with keywords in their comparison of English and French extremist texts. As they argue, '[m]ethodologically, the examination of cross-linguistic categories rather than words allowed us to examine broader trends and the ways in which meanings can be expressed in a range of different ways in both languages' (Baker & Vessey, 2018: 275). However, even this approach ultimately relies on identifying (near) translation equivalents (Baker & Vessey, 2018: 261). Our own approach takes as a starting point referring expressions used in the Chinese dataset to refer to the Chinese national day, and referring expressions used in the Australian dataset to refer to the Australian national day. These expressions are hence not strictly speaking translation equivalents, since they refer to two different referents, the Chinese national day and the Australian national day. This is different to, say, an analysis of how

Table 1.8 A sample of cross-linguistic corpus-assisted discourse studies

Study	Languages compared	Equivalents used for corpus construction and/or corpus linguistic analysis
Xiao & McEnery (2006)	English, Chinese	Groups of near synonyms relating to consequence, cause, and price/cost, for example *result/outcome/ jie2guo3* (结果); *consequence/ aftermath/ hou4guo3* (后果) and others (*cheng2guo3* (成果) 'achievement'; *shuo4guo3* (硕果) 'great achievement', *ku3guo3* (苦果) 'a bitter pill to swallow' ; *e4guo3* (恶果) 'evil consequence')
Grundmann & Krishnamurthy (2010)	English, German, French	*climate change, global warming, greenhouse effect/Klimawandel, globale Erwärmung, Treibhauseffekt, Klimakatastrophe/ changement climatique, effet de serre, réchauffement de la planète, réchauffement climatique*
Jaworska & Krishnamurthy (2012)	English, German	*feminism/Feminismus*
Taylor (2014)	English, Italian	*refugee*, asylum seeker*, immigrant*, migrant*/immigrat*, clandestin*, extracomunitar*, stranier**

the seventieth anniversary of the foundation of the People's Republic of China in 2019 was represented in Chinese vs. Australian newspapers. In addition, the referring expressions were **not** used as seed words in the corpus-building phase and arose from analysis of the data as well as from researcher familiarity with the cultural context (see Sections 2 and 3).

The focus of most cross-linguistic corpus-assisted discourse studies is on identifying representations, discourses, thematic categories, or the profiles of specific words (e.g. their semantic prosody). In contrast, we focus mainly on the news values constructed in the co-text of the respective referring expressions. This aligns us with Fruttaldo and Venuti's (2017) cross-cultural DNVA, although their analysis is 'manual' rather than corpus-assisted.

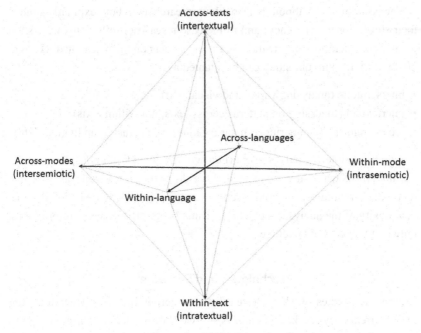

Figure 1.2 A three-dimensional topology for situating research

Furthermore, we bring in analysis of two different semiotic modes, analysing both verbal text and visual text (news photographs). To explain the focus of our study further, we will use the three-dimensional topology in Figure 1.2, a modification of an earlier version introduced in Bednarek and Caple (2017). The topology focuses on scalar distinctions between different foci of research. The relevant distinctions are

a) on the horizontal axis: whether the study focuses on one semiotic mode (intrasemiotic/monomodal) or more than one (intersemiotic/multimodal),
b) on the vertical axis: whether the primary focus of the study is on patterns **across** texts (intertextual) or patterns **within** texts (intratextual), and
c) on the oblique axis: whether the study focuses on one language or is cross-linguistic.

These parameters intersect, producing zones of analysis. For instance, the cross-linguistic corpus-assisted discourse studies reviewed previously can simultaneously be positioned as intrasemiotic (monomodal), intertextual, and 'across-languages'. To clarify, studies interested in intertextual patterns focus on patterns or trends across several texts in a corpus, while studies interested in intratextual patterns focus on the development of meaning within individual texts. Cross-linguistic studies analyse more than one language.

The point of such a topology is to allow researchers to both explicitly situate their study (for transparency) and to increase researcher reflexivity, that is, 'a greater consideration of how the researcher impacts on the researched' (Baker, 2012: 255). In sum, our study can be situated as:

- intersemiotic (analysing verbal and visual text),
- intertextual (focussing on patterns across texts, not within texts),
- cross-linguistic (comparing Mandarin Chinese with Australian English data).

This focus on intertextual patterns brings with it certain limitations; thus, we do not undertake whole-text analysis and we do not systematically analyse the text–image relations that hold within a given multimodal text. Finally, the complexity of the analysis necessitates a small dataset, and we therefore focus only on two years of coverage.

Techniques and Software

In previous studies, we have tested different corpus linguistic techniques for DNVA: frequency and keyness analysis of word forms, lemmas, n-grams, part-of-speech tags or semantic tags as well as collocation and word sketch analysis. We found that qualitative analysis of concordance lines was crucial. In this Element, we therefore rely largely on analysis of concordances, guided by some analysis of word frequency and collocation. We use word frequency lists to identify which referring expressions are common in the two datasets. We use collocation analysis to identify the different labels in the Australian dataset by examining and visualising collocates of *day* (see Section 3). Collocation analysis proceeds by taking a word (the *node*, i.e. *day*) and identifying which other words typically co-occur with it in a given co-textual span. These co-occurring words are called *collocates* and are discovered with the help of collocation measures, which identify collocates by comparing how often they are **expected** to co-occur with the word of interest with how often they **actually** occur (Brezina et al., 2015: 144).

We also report on the 'range' (Nation & Waring, 1997) of word forms or collocations where relevant, that is, their distribution across articles within the corpus. Finally, it is possible to identify words or expressions that may potentially establish newsworthiness (e.g. the adjective *shocking* may construct Unexpectedness, while *first* can construe Timeliness or Unexpectedness). Such forms are labelled 'pointers' to newsworthiness (Bednarek & Caple, 2014: 145). However, only qualitative analysis of concordance lines can tell us whether any news values are established in a given instance. Consider the use of *first* in Figure 1.3, for example: In lines 1 and 2, it is used to refer to the *First*

1   Aboriginal people. "We understand on this day 229 years ago the coming of the First Fleet wreaked a terrible impact on your people, your families, your culture," he
2   to ignore or 'whitewash Australia's dark past' and the injustices committed against the first Australians," and added that the two girls whose image attracted an Islamophobic
3   house. It's not creepy. It's beautiful, it's like him. He is here, but not here." Batty is the first ordinary Australian to be appointed Australian of the Year. She wasn't famous
4   late yesterday, forcing the cancellation of the city's Australia Day fireworks for the first time in the 32-year history of an event that was expected to attract 300,000 people.

Figure 1.3 Different uses of *first*

Fleet and the *first Australians* respectively and does not establish any news-worthiness. In contrast, in line 3, *first* establishes Timeliness (newness – the first time this has ever happened), while in line 4, it constructs Timeliness and possibly also Unexpectedness (unusuality – the first time in 32 years).

The concordance view presented in Figure 1.3 is called a KWIC view and displays a limited co-text, although we always analyse full sentences. Whether we present full sentences or concordance lines in this Element, note that we often focus on a particular news value when discussing examples. So when we provide a particular example for the construction of Negativity, for instance, we do **not** describe all of the other news values that are **also** constructed in this example. Thus, in Figure 1.3 news values other than Timeliness or Unexpectedness are clearly established (albeit not through the use of *first*). In sum, in our concordance analysis in this Element we carry out discursive news values analysis of the complete sentence where our search term appears, expanding the co-text further where necessary (in the case of anaphoric reference, for instance). We then classify all of the news values that are constructed in the relevant sentence (using Table 1.2 as a general guide, but not as a checklist), allowing multiple categories for the same language resource where appropriate.

The programs we use for corpus linguistic analysis are WordSmith (Scott, 2017–2019), Lancsbox/GraphColl (Brezina et al., 2015), MyZiCiFreqTool (Jin et al., 2005), and SysConc (Wu, 2009). MyZiCiFreqTool (developed by the Institute of Applied Linguistics, Ministry of Education, P.R. China) was chosen because a previous study (Huan, 2018) found that it outperformed other corpus tools such as AntConc (Anthony, 2016) and WordSmith on Chinese data.[7] Because MyZiCiFreqTool can only calculate the frequency of Chinese words, rather than producing concordances, we used SysConc to extract concordances. For the visual DNVA, we used an MS Excel spreadsheet. The photographs in the ChinaDay corpus were screen captured from the newspapers' online news portals, as recorded in the Database of Chinese Key Newspapers. The photographs in the AusDay corpus were also screen captured, either from microfiche copies of the newspapers held by the State Library of New South Wales (2016 AusDay data) or from the physical copy of the newspapers (2017 AusDay data). The spreadsheets for visual DNVA included publication information, bylines,

---

[7] The tool can be retrieved at http://corpus.zhonghuayuwen.org/Resources.aspx.

and captions to the photographs, where available. The construal of each news value in the photographs was recorded in the spreadsheet.

Caveats about Cross-Linguistic Analysis

When undertaking cross-linguistic discourse analysis it is important **not** to assign primacy to a language-specific framework and use this to analyse all languages. The framework for linguistic analysis introduced in Table 1.2 applies only to English-language news. For other languages, it is necessary to independently develop an inventory of linguistic resources. In our case, we took the ten news values (rather than the linguistic resources) as our departure point, and Changpeng Huan inductively established whether and how these values are constructed in the Chinese data. There is still the basic assumption, however, that the list of these news values is relevant to the Chinese news context. In addition, it is clear that more work is necessary to develop an inventory for Chinese, as we focus more on the results in this Element than on the resources, and as our analysis is limited to a specific case study.

In relation to the visual analysis of news photographs, the situation is slightly different, as the technical resources for taking photographs would be the same across both cultures. Nevertheless, cultural differences may exist in relation to how photographs are read and understood. As further explained in Section 2, we therefore tested whether the inventory of visual resources in Table 1.2 can be applied to the Chinese data, and to do so, we discussed photographs with a variety of Chinese nationals (including Changpeng Huan).

In carrying out corpus-assisted multimodal discourse analysis of news coverage of the national days of China and Australia, we aim to answer the following questions:

- What news values are discursively construed in different cultures around a similar event?
- How are these values typically constructed?
- How does the construction of newsworthiness relate to national identity?
- What are the similarities and differences in what the corpus linguistic analysis uncovers and what the visual analysis uncovers?

While our analysis in this Element focuses on multimodal discourse (language and image as used in published news items), we will occasionally draw on non-linguistic aspects in our interpretation, such as differences between the two countries (China and Australia) or differences between newspapers where these appear striking (*People's Daily* and *Nanfang Metro*). In Section 2, we present our analysis of the construction of news values in relation to China's national day. In Section 3, we then do the same for Australia's national day. Section 4 will provide a synthesis and comparison of results. We also reflect upon our approach to corpus-assisted multimodal discourse analysis.

2 China National Day: Copied and Commercialised

2.1 Using Corpus Linguistics to Analyse the ChinaDay Corpus

Our first study focuses on the Chinese national day. Displays of patriotism towards the nation play a central role in national day celebrations in China and in the analysis presented in this section we aim to uncover the extent to which this is reflected in the news reporting. Discursive news values analysis of both the verbal and visual reporting of the national day celebrations in China are presented in turn. The analysis is an example of CAMDA, since it draws on corpus linguistic techniques to assess the linguistic resources in Chinese that construct news values. This corpus-based discourse analysis is complemented by qualitative analysis of the photographs for the construal of newsworthiness, making our analysis multimodal.

We began our interrogation of the ChinaDay corpus by identifying the major terms that refer to the national day in China (using a frequency list[8]), and then moved on to close examination of how newsworthiness is constructed around these terms using concordance analysis. In this analysis we draw on corpus linguistic software that has been developed specifically for use with simplified Chinese characters (introduced in Section 1).

2.1.1 Identifying Node Words and their Newsworthiness

Since Australia Day is referred to in several different ways (see Sections 1 and 3), we wanted to assess whether the same is true for the Chinese national day. To do this we examined the top 200 most frequent words in the ChinaDay corpus using MyZiCiFreqTool (Jin et al., 2005). Because of differences between English and Chinese, using collocation analysis to identify national day labels (as we do for the Australian data) is not appropriate. To identify additional terms, we also drew on Changpeng Huan's familiarity with the corpus texts, as well as with the cultural context. Six node words that refer to the national day were identified. These are listed in Table 2.1. *Huangjinzhou* (黄金周, 'golden week'), *huadan* (华诞) and *shengri* (生日) were identified through close reading of the texts and do not appear in the top 200 most frequent items. The term *huangjinzhou* (黄金周, 'golden week') encompasses the fact that this Chinese holiday extends over a week. To

[8] The word frequency list of the ChinaDay corpus is provided in Appendix 1 in the online appendices at Cambridge University Press, www.cambridge.org/9781108814072.

Table 2.1 The investigated expressions referring to the national day with their frequency and range

Node words	Pinyin	English translation	Frequency	Range
国庆	guoqing	national celebration	458	191
黄金周	huangjinzhou	golden week	160	180
十一	shiyi	October 1	24	23
周年	zhounian	anniversary	45	39
生日/华诞	shengri/huadan	birthday	25	22

clarify, the frequencies we provide in Table 2.1 do not correspond to the frequency in the form-based frequency list, but rather only include those occurrences where the words actually refer to the national day. This explains why *huangjinzhou* (黄金周) has a higher frequency than words from the top 200 (十一/*shiyi* and 周年/*zhounian*).[9]

We first identified how newsworthiness is encapsulated through the labels themselves. For example, Timeliness is constructed in the labels *guoqing* (国庆), *huangjinzhou* (黄金周) and *shiyi* (十一). Since the design of our dataset used time as a variable (collecting articles within a one-week span of the national day), and since these labels therefore automatically construct Timeliness, we do not analyse the corpus any further for this news value. Positivity is also constructed in *guoqing* (国庆) and *huangjinzhou* (黄金周) through their compounding with 'celebration' and 'golden', and Proximity is constructed in *guoqing* (国庆) through 'national', referring to the Chinese nation. As we will see in Section 3, labels like *Invasion Day* and *Survival Day* referencing the Australian national day construct Negativity. However, none of the labels used to refer to the Chinese national day construct this news value.

Another general observation worthy of elaboration in relation to the ChinaDay corpus is that of press censorship in China. This is because this impacts on the results both across newspapers investigated in this study and across the years of reporting we collected. When reporting on the activities of political leaders during national day celebrations, the language in both *People's*

---

[9] A more detailed description of how these six node words were identified and distinguished from other related word forms is given in Appendix 2 in the online appendices, www.cambridge.org/9781108814072.

Daily and *Nanfang Metro* is identical, as demonstrated in Examples 1 and 2 from each of these newspapers:[10]

EX 1. 习近平、李克强、张德江、刘云山、王岐山、张高丽等党和国家领导人
      与1100多位中外人士欢聚一堂，共庆共和国华诞。PP15016[11]

   Xi Jinping, Li Keqiang, Zhang Dejiang, Liu Yunshan, Wang Qishan, and
   Zhang Gaoli, leaders of the country and CCP, happily gathered together with
   more than 1,100 domestic and international guests to celebrate the birth of the
   Republic.

EX 2. 习近平、李克强、张德江、刘云山、王岐山、张高丽等党和国家领导人
      与1100多位中外人士欢聚一堂，共庆共和国华诞。NM15025

   Xi Jinping, Li Keqiang, Zhang Dejiang, Liu Yunshan, Wang Qishan, and
   Zhang Gaoli, leaders of the country and CCP, happily gathered together with
   more than 1,100 domestic and international guests to celebrate the birth of the
   Republic.

This wholesale copying of content is largely due to press censorship in China, where news reporting involving political elites must be reviewed and overseen by the Ministry of Publicity at corresponding national or local government levels (Huan, 2016). Previous ethnographic research observing news production processes in a local Chinese newspaper (Huan, 2016, 2018) found that local newspapers rely heavily, if not totally, on news feeds from the Big Three, namely *Xinhua*, *People's Daily*, and *CCTV* to fill in their sections of national and international news. More importantly, reporters only retain the power to revise such news through deletion and integration (e.g. mixing reports on the same event from the Big Three). There are even clear linguistic devices to distinguish sources that are the exact reproduction of one of the Big Three from those that are mixed and integrated. Specifically, if a report begins or ends with 据新华社报道 (*ju Xinhuashe baodao*, meaning 'according to *Xinhua* news'), then it signals an integrated report; by contrast, without the first Chinese character 据(*ju*), the news at issue is an exact reproduction from *Xinhua*.

Perhaps a more alarming observation of the Chinese reporting (from a 'Western-centric' perspective) is the fact that identical wording and sentence structures are used across the two years of reporting on the national day in the ChinaDay corpus. In examples 3 and 4 (from 2015 and 2016 respectively, and published in *People's Daily*), only the name and role of the national leader (Liu

---

[10] All Chinese examples in this section were translated by Changpeng Huan. The translation is 'free', rather than 'literal', with changes to sentence structure, etc.

[11] The ID numbers listed next to the examples indicate which newspaper they are from [PP=*People's Daily*; NM=*Nanfang Metro*], the year of publication [15=2015; 16=2016] and the text number, e.g. 016.

Yunshan in EX3, and Yu Zhengsheng in EX4) and the year of anniversary are different (underlined in the translated text), while the rest, including the number of invited guests, remains identical:

EX 3. 中共中央政治局常委、中央书记处书记刘云山与2800余名港澳台侨各界代表欢聚一堂，共同庆祝中华人民共和国成立66周年。PP15008

> Liu Yunshan, member of the Standing Committee of the Political Bureau of the CPC Central Committee and secretary of the Central Secretariat, and more than 2,800 representatives from various circles of Hong Kong, Macau and Taiwan have gathered together to celebrate the 66th anniversary of the founding of the People's Republic of China.

EX 4. 中共中央政治局常委、全国政协主席俞正声与2800多名港澳台侨各界代表欢聚一堂，庆祝中华人民共和国成立67周年。PP16003

> Yu Zhengsheng, member of the Standing Committee of the Political Bureau of the CPC Central Committee and chairman of the National Committee of the Chinese People's Political Consultative Conference, and more than 2,800 representatives from various circles of Hong Kong, Macau and Taiwan have gathered to celebrate the 67th anniversary of the founding of the People's Republic of China.

These factors would impact significantly on any attempt to quantify all instances of the construction of news values in the ChinaDay corpus. We therefore report only on tendencies rather than reporting exact percentages or figures in the following (in contrast to the *Australia Day* analysis in Section 3). The copying of content on such a large scale means that there is very little variety in the kinds of news values constructed. Next, we examine how newsworthiness is constructed in relation to the Chinese national day using concordances of the node words identified. The focus of our analysis is on the close co-text of the various labels for the national day, with the full sentence acting as the unit of analysis.

2.1.2 Major News Values in the ChinaDay Corpus

Using the software tool SysConc (Wu, 2009) to generate concordances of the selected node words referring to the national day, we analyzed the sentences in which these node words occur. We were mainly interested in identifying the patterns in news value construction, and the linguistic resources used to realise these news values. One of the key observations we can make is that the same four news values are consistently constructed in relation to the national day, no matter which label is being used. These are Proximity, Positivity, Superlativeness and Eliteness (see Figure 2.1). For this reason, we first address

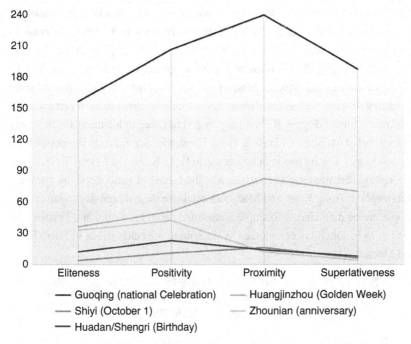

Figure 2.1 The main four news values constructed in relation to each of the labels referencing the national day (raw numbers)

each of these four dominant news values in turn rather than deal with each node word in turn. Other news values are then briefly discussed in Section 2.1.3.

Another general observation that emerges from the concordance analysis is the fact that the two newspapers investigated for this study draw on different linguistic resources to construct Proximity and Eliteness. Being a national newspaper targeting officials at different levels of government across China, *People's Daily* mainly references nationally recognised places and politicians. *Nanfang Metro*, however, mainly targets readers from the Guangdong/Pearl River Delta region – including the Special Administrative Regions (SARs) of Hong Kong and Macau. Therefore, *Nanfang Metro* principally references local elite news actors and places known to the newspaper's target market. This means there is a national/local divide in the construction of the news values of Proximity and Eliteness, except when the content is simply copied from official, national news agencies, which is sometimes the case when the reporting includes the actions and activities of the top political elites (cf. Sun, 2012).

Proximity

The linguistic markers of Proximity in the ChinaDay corpus mainly consist of references to places and institutions known to the target audiences. We also found that this news value tends to co-occur with Positivity, especially in relation to descriptions of actions and activities that signify unity and a sense of pride in nationhood. The naming of locations such as 天安门广场 (Tian'anmen Square, Beijing), 香港金紫荆广场 (Golden Bauhinia Square, Hong Kong), and 金莲花 广场 (Golden Lotus Square, Macau) (in EX5), construct the news value of Proximity for Chinese readers. References to locations closer to the target audience construct a higher degree of Proximity than references to locations further away and not part of mainland China (e.g. Hong Kong, Macau), although this depends on the newspaper. The inclusion of references to Hong Kong and Macau in relation to flag-raising ceremonies also construct a unified sense of nationhood, by implying that people in Hong Kong and Macau all celebrate the national day together with people on the mainland.[12] Example 5 constructs both Proximity and Positivity in relation to national day ceremonies by describing the celebrations in Hong Kong and Macau:

EX 5. **香港特区政府**于1日清晨在**金紫荆广场**举行隆重升旗仪式，约2500名香港 社会各界人士到场观礼；**澳门特区政府**在**金莲花广场**举行隆重升旗仪 式，逾千人一同观礼，共庆新中国67周年华诞。PP16020

> The Hong Kong SAR Government held a grand flag-raising ceremony at the Golden Bauhinia Square on the early morning of October 1st. About 2,500 people from all walks of life in Hong Kong attended the ceremony. The Macau SAR Government held a grand flag-raising ceremony at the Golden Lotus Plaza. More than 1,000 people attended the ceremony to celebrate the 67th anniversary of the new China.

Other linguistic resources that construct Proximity include possessive determiners when coupled with references to China as the motherland (我们伟大祖国 / *our great motherland*), as in example 6. This compounding of place with positive evaluation further combines Proximity and Positivity, creating a feeling of pride in the nation, which, as we will see throughout the section, emerges as an underlying theme of the reporting.

EX 6. 我特意把你们请过来，来京参加国庆活动，共同庆祝**我们伟大祖国**的生 日。PP15015

> I specially invited you to come to Beijing to participate in the National Day celebration to celebrate the birthday of our great motherland.

---

[12] Sovereignty over Hong Kong and Macau was transferred to China in 1997 and 1999 respectively. However, these two SARs maintain capitalist systems, while China 'has been transformed from a planned economy into a [socialist] market economy' (Shi-xu, 2014: 63). This constitutes the basic tenet of *One Country, Two Systems*, in that Hong Kong, Macau and mainland China maintain two different systems of capitalism and socialism, while belonging to one China in terms of sovereignty.

An example of the local focus of *Nanfang Metro* can be seen in example 7, where Proximity is constructed for local readers through reference to the Changlong Zoo. Again, Proximity co-occurs with Positivity through the repetition of 国宝 (*national treasure*), and 开趴 (*held a party to celebrate*). That these are 'national' treasures all coming together to celebrate another nation again points to the centrality of pride in the nation and nationhood in the reporting.

EX 7. 我国国宝大熊猫三胞胎、澳大利亚国宝考拉、马来西亚国宝黄猩猩、印度国宝白虎、泰国国宝亚洲象......80多个国家的动物国宝们，在长隆野生动物世界为新中国成立66周年开趴。NM15014

> China's national treasure giant panda triplets, Australian national treasure koalas, Malaysian national treasures, yellow gorillas, Indian national treasures, white tigers, Thai national treasures, Asian elephants ... National treasured animals from more than 80 countries in the Changlong Wildlife Zoo, held a party to celebrate the 66th anniversary of the new China.

Overall, Proximity is mainly constructed through explicit references to geographically close places, local communities or government sections, and well-known airlines (e.g. 南航/Southern China Airline) or train stations (e.g. 广州南站/South Guangzhou Station). Again, *Nangfang Metro* predominantly adopts references to local places that are geographically close to Guangzhou, including references to its administrative towns or districts (e.g. 花都区/Huadu District), local parks (e.g. 雁鸣湖/Yanming Lak), nearby cities in Guandong (e.g. 佛山市/Foshan City, 东莞市/Dongguan City, 珠海市/Zhuhai City), local train stations (e.g. 广州南站/South Guangzhou Station), and places in Hong Kong (e.g. 香港铜锣湾/Tongluowan in Hong Kong). In contrast, *People's Daily* refers to more diverse places across China, mainly including the names of capital cities or provinces.

Positivity

The examples presented so far have already shown us a number of ways in which Positivity is constructed in relation to the Chinese national day. This can be through positive emotions (e.g. 高兴/'happily', or 庆祝/'celebrate'), or positive evaluative language (e.g. 伟大/'great' – referring to the motherland). Another example (EX8), in relation to the label 生日/'birthday', includes the use of 热情洋溢/'enthusiastic', 掌声/'applause' and 欢呼声/'cheers', to refer to the positive emotions and actions of the people as they celebrate the day:

EX 8. 热情洋溢的人们用歌声、掌声、欢呼声迎来共和国的生日。PP15028

> Enthusiastic people celebrate the birthday of the Republic with songs, applause, and cheers.

Descriptions of positive behaviour in relation to national day activities and events play a central role in the construction of Positivity and appear to reinforce valued behaviours associated with the event. These constructions of Positivity further contribute to instilling in readers a sense of pride in the nation. Examples of positive behaviour include attending flag-raising ceremonies (see EX5), attending special receptions at overseas embassies (EX9 – demonstrating the good behaviour of Chinese nationals living overseas), volunteering across a range of activities including raising awareness of public safety (EX10), or spending the national holiday accompanying lonely seniors or struggling families (EX11).

EX 9. 中国驻德国大使馆在9月29日和30日两天，分别举办华侨华人专场招待会和国庆66周年招待会。PP15026

On September 29th and 30th, the Chinese Embassy in Germany held a special reception for overseas Chinese to celebrate the 66th anniversary of the National Day.

EX 10. 29日，山东诸城市善小志愿服务队的志愿者们走进密州街道王铁小学，开展"十一"国庆放假期间安全常识宣讲活动。PP16009

On the 29th, volunteers from Shanxiao Volunteer Service Team, Zhucheng City, Shandong Province, went to Wangtie Primary School in Mizhou Street to publicise public safety during the "October 1" National Day holiday.

EX 11. "十一"长假期间，不少高校心理学院的学生们，也走进失独家庭、留守儿童家中，陪他们聊天、解闷……各地群众自发组织的志愿行动，传递着暖意，构成节假日的一道独特风景。PP15047

During the "11" holiday, many college students majoring in psychology visited the families of the disabled and left-behind children, chatting with them, and relieving them. Their actions make you feel warm, bringing a special holiday spirit to the picture.

It is not just ordinary citizens whose positive behaviour (patriotism or service to others) is described. The positive actions of authorities are also described, including devising initiatives to ease traffic congestion (EX12), or to improve the flow of travellers (EX13) during the holidays. Descriptions of officials who stay on in their posts and sacrifice their own holiday for the good of others also occur (through lexis such as 24 小时值班/on duty 24 hours). The national day is also associated with benefits or freedoms such as free entry to museums, the possibility of taking (overseas) holidays, removing the highway tolls, or offering promotions and discounts to shoppers (as exemplified in EX14).

EX 12. 为方便广大驾驶人，缓解交通拥堵，东莞交警将在十一期间，联合路政
和三大保险公司，在高速路服务区、出口处等地，**设立5个快处快赔点。**
NM15021

In order to facilitate the majority of drivers and ease traffic congestion, the
Dongguan traffic police will set up five fast-track compensation points during
the October 1 holiday, in conjunction with the road administration and the three
major insurance companies, in the service areas and exits of the expressway.

EX 13. 高铁不仅让城市之间往来**更便捷，**还串起多个旅游景区，为黄金周铁路
客流井喷**提供了充足动力。**PP15050

The high-speed railway not only makes the exchanges between cities more
convenient, but also connects many tourist attractions, which provides suffi-
cient momentum for the passenger flow during the Golden Week.

EX 14. 一说到"十一"，很多人会一下子联想到"黄金周"长假，眼前浮现的是"假
日出境游""自驾游攻略""**高速不收费**""**商场大降价**".....PP16005

When it comes to "October 1", many people will suddenly think of the
"Golden Week" holiday, and the "holiday outbound tour", "self-driving
tour guide", "free-of-charge highway" and "big promotions" ...

Superlativeness

Superlativeness is constructed through references to the boost to the national
economy that is brought about by the increased movement of tourists along with
the promotion of shopping during the holiday week. Lexis identifying booming
revenues along with quantifiers referring to income and passenger movement
construct Superlativeness in examples 15 and 16, while example 17 includes a
reference to the large numbers of volunteers.

EX 15. 据北京市旅游委统计，2015年"十一"假期，首都北京共接待旅游者**1151.6
万人次，**比去年同期增长**1.6%，**旅游总收入**82.1亿元，**同比增长**7.1%。**
PP15074

According to the statistics released by the Beijing Tourism Administration,
during the "October 1" holiday in 2015, Beijing received a total of 11.516
million tourists, an increase of 1.6% over the same period of last year. The
total tourism revenue was 8.31 billion yuan, a year-on-year increase of 7.1%.

EX 16. 据了解，麦当劳、肯德基等快餐企业黄金周营业额超**1.2亿元，增幅达两
位数。**NM15044

It is reported that the turnover of McDonald's, KFC and other fast-food
enterprises in the Golden Week exceeded 120 million yuan, an increase of
around 10%.

EX 17. 该地旅游协会工作人员于志明介绍，超**5000人次**志愿者服务国庆黄金周，政府部门**24小时**值班。PP16049

> Yu Zhiming, a staff member of the local tourism association said, more than 5,000 volunteers served the National Day Golden Week, and the government department was on duty 24 hours a day.

Comparisons to previous years (EXs 18–20), indicating increased tourist movement, business transaction and revenues, also construe Superlativeness, especially when the increase is constructed as record-breaking (EX18 and EX19).

EX 18. 南都记者从广州南站获悉，今年"十一"长假期间，车站迎来开通以来最大客流，9月28日至10月7日预计10天发送旅客**175万人**，日均发送**17.5万人**，同比增长**4%**，刷新历史纪录。[NM16026]

> Reporters of Nanfang Metro learned from Guangzhou South Railway Station that during the "October 1" holiday this year, the station ushered in the largest passenger flow since its opening. From September 28 to October 7, it is expected to send 1.75 million passengers in 10 days, with an average daily delivery of 175,000, an increase of 4% year-on-year, setting a new record.

EX 19. 从广梅汕铁路部门得到消息，今年国庆运输期间，广梅汕铁路共计发送旅客约**30万人次**，同比2014年增加**1 .4万人次**，增长**4 .87%**；日均发送旅客**4.4万人次**，创黄金周运输历史纪录；最高单日(10月2日)发送旅客**5.2万人次**，增长**11.86%**。NM15057

> According to the news from the Guangzhou-Meizhou Railway Department, during the National Day transportation period, the Guangzhou-Meizhou-Shantou Railway sent a total of 300,000 passengers, an increase of 14,000 passengers (or 4.87%) from 2014, an average of 44,000 passengers per day. The number of visits set the new record of the Golden Week transportation; the peak day (October 2) sent 52,000 passengers, an increase of 11.86%

EX 20. 黄金周期间，三亚全市接待游客**61.23万人次**，同比增长**21.01%**。PP16049

> During the Golden Week, Sanya received 612,300 tourists, a year-on-year increase of 21.01%.

The newspapers' focus on tourism and the turnover of revenues in relation to entertainment and spending, often using figures released by elite institutions (government sections in most cases), also points to the fact that the national day is not just a day to celebrate nationhood and to display patriotism, but has also increasingly come to be seen as a commercialised holiday period in which big spending and high tourist movement are also celebrated.

Eliteness

Moving on to the fourth major news value we identified, many examples of the construction of Eliteness have already appeared in the examples above. The political elite, often accompanied by their title/role, are named along with the activities they are engaged in during national day ceremonies (EXs 3 and 4). Elite institutional authorities, especially the 旅游委/'tourism administration' (EX15), 铁路部门/'transport authorities' (EX19) or 东莞交警/'traffic police in Dongguan' (EX12) are also named as the providers of statistics and information on tourism income and the movement of tourists over the holiday period. Other elites (e.g. Chai Laiyi, the deputy president of the Polish Senate), are named as they express congratulations and send good wishes to the nation (EX21).

EX 21. 柴莱伊热烈祝贺中华人民共和国成立67周年，对中国取得的巨大成就表示由衷钦佩，真诚祝愿波中两国人民的友谊世代相传。PP16015

> Chai Laiyi [the deputy president of the Polish Senate] warmly congratulated the People's Republic of China on its 67th anniversary and expressed sincere admiration for China's tremendous achievements. He sincerely hoped that the friendship between the two peoples will be passed down from generation to generation.

The local/national focus of the reporting in *Nanfang Metro* and *People's Daily* is reflected in the types of elites that are referenced. *Nanfang Metro* mainly references elite sources from the local 旅游局/'tourism administration', 统计局/'statistics bureau', 广州站/'Guangzhou railway stations', and the 香港商业与经济发展局/'Commerce and Economic Development Bureau of the Hong Kong Special Administrative Region'. In contrast, *People's Daily* draws on elite news sources representing the higher level state administrations of commerce, transportation (国家铁路总局/'National Railway Administration', 中国民航总局/'Civil Aviation Administration of China'), tourism (国家文化与旅游部/'Ministry of Culture and Tourism'), media and entertainment (广电总局/'State Administration of Press, Publication, Radio, Film, and Television'), and security (公安部/'Ministry of Public Security'), as well as 故宫/'the Forbidden City'.

As noted, the reporting of figures provided by these elite organs of the State suggests a growing importance being placed on the economic value of the national day. In addition, there is a focus on the political elite and their expressions of patriotism and pride in the nation enacted in national day ceremonies.

2.1.3 Other News Value Constructions and National Day Reporting

Other news values (e.g. Negativity, Impact, Personalisation) are also constructed in the ChinaDay corpus. However, they occur much less frequently than the four major news values just discussed. The construction of Negativity is associated with descriptions of declining revenues that some sectors of the economy suffered during the national holiday week. Example 22 construes Negativity by pointing to falling revenues in the hotel sector in Hong Kong, citing falls of 15–20 per cent, and stating that 再难以出现往日黄金周一房难求的盛况/*the heyday of over-booked hotels during the Golden week in the past has gone*.[13] The increase in traffic flow during the national holiday is also associated with security risks and congestion (EX23). Negativity is also established in the reporting of deaths related to the bad behaviour of motorists (occupying the emergency lanes on the highway and thus blocking access for emergency response teams), as shown in example 24. In *Nanfang Metro* tropical disease outbreaks during the national holiday week (EX25) are reported on, accompanied by advice on how to remain safe/protected against infection.

EX 22. 黄金周期间香港酒店业平均房租**下跌15%至20%**，但入住率却维持在80%至90%水平，**再难出现**以往黄金周一房难求的盛况。NM15056.

During the Golden Week, the average rent of the hotel industry in Hong Kong fell by 15% to 20%, but the occupancy rate remained at 80% to 90%. The heyday of over-booked hotels during the Golden Week in the past has gone.

EX 23. 据介绍，今年"十一"国庆假期全国道路交通流量同比上升12%以上，一些重点地区甚至高达20%以上，**安全风险加大，疏堵压力增大**。PP15071

According to reports, in this year's "October 1" National Day holiday, national road traffic flow increased by more than 12% year-on-year, and some key areas even increased by more than 20%, thus increasing security risks and congestion pressure.

EX 24. 浙江境内一司机因为应急车道被占**得不到及时救援而身亡**，福建境内一女士也因同样情况而**导致流产、生命垂危**……国庆假期，多起因挤占应急车道影响救援的事件让人扼腕。PP15072

A driver in Zhejiang has died because the emergency lane was occupied and he was not able to receive timely medical treatment. A woman in Fujian also had a miscarriage and eventually died due to the same situation … during the National Day holiday, sadly many incidents were caused by the occupation of the emergency lane.

---

[13] Hong Kong was once popular and famous among people from mainland China for its scenery and tax-free shopping centres. However, there was a heightened wave of anti-mainland China movement in 2015 in Hong Kong, triggered by increasing numbers of travellers from mainland China, and resentment towards those who only came to Hong Kong to stock up on baby formula. This movement provoked immense aversion towards citizens in mainland China, resulting in a decline in mainland Chinese travelling to and shopping in Hong Kong. As most people would travel to Hong Kong from Guangzhou or Shenzhen, this decline is mainly reported in *Nanfang Metro*.

EX 25. 尤其在中秋、国庆期间往来目前广东省登革热疫情严重的地区如潮州等地，应注意防止蚊虫叮咬。NM15001

> During the Mid-Autumn Festival and National Day, there is a serious epidemic of dengue fever in Guangdong Province, especially in Chaozhou, visitors need to pay special attention to preventing mosquito bites.

The news value of Impact, which constructs events in terms of their (significant) consequences, often co-occurs with Negativity (and is affected by the material reality of events). In 2015, the national day holiday was affected by typhoon activity in Guangdong province, which had significant negative effects on tourist attractions in the region (EX26). The congestion on the highways was also reported as a negative consequence of travellers still returning from the national holidays (EX27 and EX23).

EX 26. 国庆黄金周受强台风"彩虹"在广东地区登陆影响，广州主要旅游景区接待经营情况出现下滑。NM1504

> The National Day Golden Week was affected by the landing of strong typhoon "Rainbow" in Guangdong, and the reception and operation of major tourist attractions in Guangzhou declined.

EX 27. 明日(10月8日)是国庆黄金周后首个工作日，受工作日通勤交通与假期返程客流叠加影响，市交委预计当日全市交通拥堵情况相比节前有所加剧，市区将有十条主干道拥堵。NM15043

> Tomorrow (October 8th) is the first working day after the National Day Golden Week. Due to the overlapping of commuter traffic and holiday passengers returning on the working day, the Municipal Traffic Commission expects that the traffic congestion in the city will be intensified compared with that before the holiday. There will be congestion of ten main roads in the urban area.

Also surprisingly infrequent in the ChinaDay corpus are constructions of Personalisation. This news value is construed by reference to ordinary Chinese citizens through the use of their names and kinship relationships (EX28). The narration of personal stories like those about national day experiences under the headline 'My National Day Memories' not only construct Personalisation, but also promote a sense of national belonging through shared national day memories.

EX 28. 今年国庆黄金周，梁广源没有安排出游计划，他一脸认真地对南都记者说，准备带着孙子，在家中玩《血战上海滩》电脑游戏，以及看"抗日剧"打发假期。NM15027

> This year's National Day Golden Week, Liang Guangyuan did not plan to arrange travel. He said seriously to the reporter that he was ready to take his grandson to play computer games at home, and watch the "anti-Japanese drama" to kill time.

Individuals and members of minority groups who have contributed to national unity projects were recognised for their services to the nation through invitations to celebrate the national day with President Xi at the Great Hall of the People. Personalisation is construed in references to their emotional responses to these honours (EX29 about two Uighur sisters who were invited by President Xi due to their donation of a hand-made embroidery), and in being singled out, named and identified as a minority (EX30). These examples also showcase the national unity of Uighurs and people of other ethnicities in China.

EX 29. 没想到总书记还特邀**我们姐妹俩**来北京参加国庆活动，这是我们一生**最大的荣幸**。PP15015

> Unexpectedly, the General Secretary invited my sister and me to Beijing to participate in the celebration of National Day. This is the greatest honor in our life.

EX 30. 9月30日，习近平总书记在人民大会堂亲切会见了来京参加国庆活动的13名基层民族团结优秀代表，**宁夏银川市贺兰县立岗镇的秦文博**是唯一一名**回族代表**。PP15065

> On September 30, General Secretary Xi Jinping cordially met with 13 outstanding representatives of grassroots who contributed to national unity. They came to Beijing to participate in the celebration of National Day in the Great Hall of the People. Qin Wenbo, coming from Ligang Town, Helan County, Yinchuan City, Ningxia was the only representative of the Hui minority.

The results of our analysis of the construal of Unexpectedness and Consonance are not reported here because there were so few cases and there was a high level of disagreement in their interpretation.

2.1.4 Summary of the Corpus Analysis

Overall, Proximity, Positivity, Superlativeness and Eliteness are, in descending order, the most frequently constructed news values in the verbal component of the ChinaDay corpus. The presence of Positivity is not surprising, given the high levels of censorship and control exerted over content that is distributed across all new outlets by the Big Three. This also means that some of the news values in *Nanfang Metro* were largely 'copied' from *People's Daily* and there is little difference to be observed across the two in this respect. As argued elsewhere (Huan, 2016, 2018), this is the result of media censorship in China, where the image of the power elites is prudently safeguarded and overseen by the Department of Publicity at corresponding national or local levels. We now move on to the visual analysis, focusing on the news values constructed by the photographs.

2.2 Visual DNVA of the ChinaDay Corpus

As we have seen in Section 2.1, the verbal text centers on the commemorations performed by the political elites and watched by the masses, and on the movement of citizens and holidaymakers across the Golden Week, a focus that is repeated in the visual reporting of the national day holiday. While key news actors and activities are thus shared in the verbal and visual reporting, we were curious about whether the photography also mirrors the verbal text examples given in Section 2.1 in representing scenes year-on-year in almost identical compositions. Since photographers need to place themselves in amongst the action in order to capture visual representations of the national day celebrations, one might expect a much greater variety in both content and capture. We explore the extent to which this is the case and whether the same kind of restrictions and sharing of content from the Big Three are in evidence in the visual reporting.

A total of 131 photographs are associated with the verbal stories collected in the ChinaDay corpus. We analysed each photograph for the construction of news values. This analysis was collated in a MS Excel spreadsheet, noting the number of news values constructed in each photograph. The general (collated) results of this analysis are shown in Figure 2.2 (as a percentage). As with our analysis of newsworthiness in the verbal dataset, we omit Timeliness from our discussion.

For the visual DNVA, the repository of resources established by Helen Caple for DNVA in 'Anglo' news discourse (see Section 1) was used to analyse the

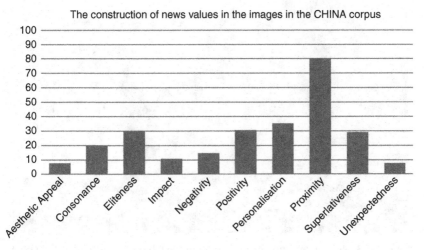

Figure 2.2 The construal of news values in the photographs in the ChinaDay corpus (as percentages)

Chinese photographs. The findings of this analysis were then discussed with Changpeng Huan. Generally, good agreement was found between both coders (Helen Caple and Changpeng Huan) regarding the visual resources for construing news values, with the main point of disagreement being in relation to uniforms as a marker of the elite status of an image participant. This will be explored in the discussion of the results concerning the construction of Eliteness later in this section. Given the much smaller data size (131 photographs), compared with the verbal corpus, it is now possible to engage more directly in the comparison of findings across the two Chinese newspapers.

Figure 2.2 shows that the photographs in the ChinaDay corpus construct the full range of news values (which is not the case in the AusDay corpus, see Figure 3.4, Section 3). The news value of Proximity (80 per cent) dominates the newsworthiness constructed in the visuals. This is also the greatest point of similarity between the two publications investigated: *People's Daily* and *Nanfang Metro*. This is followed by Personalisation (35 per cent), Positivity (31 per cent) and Eliteness (30 per cent).

Flags, signage, uniforms and landmarks widely known to the local Chinese target audiences dominate the content of the photographs, and these are all image attributes that construct Proximity (e.g. flags and signage in Example A, and well-known landmarks in Example B, Figure 2.3). Flags are also a symbol of national identity and unity and associated with nationalism and patriotism.

Figure 2.3 The construction of Proximity in the ChinaDay corpus. PHOTOS: A: *Nanfang Metro* [NM15028]; B: *Nanfang Metro* [NM15024_2]

(a)   (b)

Figure 2.4 Contrasting shot types used in the depiction of people in the ChinaDay corpus, constructing Superlativeness (A) and Personalisation (B). PHOTOS: A: *Nanfang Metro* [NM16031]; B: *People's Daily* [PP16045_1]

Interestingly, Example B in Figure 2.3 is the only photograph that is common to both *Nanfang Metro* and *People's Daily*, having been distributed by official sources (i.e. the Big Three). While photographs from the same ceremony are published by the two news outlets in both years examined in this study, this is the only photograph that is duplicated.

The construction of Personalisation differs considerably between the two news outlets studied in the ChinaDay corpus. There is a 70:30 split between *People's Daily* and *Nanfang Metro* in the construction of Personalisation. Similarly, Eliteness is much more commonly constructed in *People's Daily* (65 per cent of all instances) compared to *Nanfang Metro* (35 per cent of all instances). While both news organisations do photograph people, *People's Daily* is much more likely to focus on individuals and small groups, and to use close to mid-range shots from a frontal angle (thus constructing Personalisation), while *Nanfang Metro* makes use of very large group shots taken from a much greater distance (and more likely to construe Superlativeness). Example photographs pointing to these differences are given in Figure 2.4.

The photographs in Figure 2.4 concern Chinese people travelling home for the holidays and were captured at a transport hub. The photograph in Example A from *Nanfang Metro* is taken from a very long distance and a high, oblique angle. It captures the scope and scale of the exodus of people as they travel home for the holidays, thus construing Superlativeness.[14] The photograph in Example

---

[14] The construction of Superlativeness in Example A in Figure 2.4 was discussed by both coders. This is because it is common to see large numbers of people queuing at transport hubs throughout China on any given working day, and to a Chinese reader this might not construe Superlativeness. However, Huan explained that the scope and scale of the numbers of people in this photograph, with queues extending from every counter in the hall, and extending beyond the image frame, would indeed establish Superlativeness.

B from *People's Daily*, on the other hand, focuses on three individuals who are clearly recognisable in the photograph as they face the camera, while the 'official' helping them remains faceless. The photograph is taken from eye level to the image participants and is a mid-shot, thus enacting a social relationship between audience and image participants. Such a photograph constructs Personalisation, as individuals are singled out from the crowds to form the focus of the photograph (see description of Personalisation in Section 1).

Positivity and Eliteness are constructed in approximately 30 per cent of photographs in the ChinaDay corpus. Again, it is *People's Daily* which is far more likely to construct Positivity (70 per cent of all instances) compared with *Nanfang Metro*. The over-representation of Positivity in *People's Daily* makes sense in relation to the construction of Personalisation. In focusing on individuals at a close to social distance, as noted previously, it is more likely that audiences will be able to see and therefore gauge the emotions of image participants, which is how Positivity is commonly constructed when photographs include humans (Bednarek & Caple, 2017: 120). Eliteness is constructed through depictions not only of the political elite (e.g. Chinese President Xi Jinping and other ministers), but also of military officials and police officers. Professional elites are also photographed (e.g. medical doctors and legal professionals).

Photographs of the political elite are limited to ceremonial depictions (as in Example B in Figure 2.3) and are thus also limited to the depiction of controlled and choreographed activities. Other elites, such as military and police officers are depicted in uniform and engaging in activities that show them assisting ordinary individuals, thus further construing Positivity. Additional uniformed image participants include transport officers and food inspectors who are also depicted engaging in appropriate positive activities, such as assisting members of the public, or inspecting the quality of fresh produce. While these are also uniformed government workers, we coded these as 'weak' Eliteness. Service industry workers, such as street cleaners and information officers at transport hubs who were also uniformed were not coded as having elite status in the Chinese context.

Superlativeness is also constructed in nearly 30 per cent of all photographs, and in this case, a much higher representation of Superlativeness can be detected in the photographs from *Nanfang Metro* (70 per cent). Since *Nanfang Metro* tended to take longer shots of crowds and traffic (see Figure 2.5), this is not a surprising result. Photographs taken from a distance are able to show the scale or scope of an event (examples are given in Figure 2.5). In the photograph in Example A, the image frame is filled with people, with the vanishing point (following the line of umbrellas) tapering out towards the top

(a)   (b)

Figure 2.5 The construction of Superlativeness in photographs from *Nanfang Metro*. PHOTOS: A: *Nanfang Metro* [NM15036]; B: *Nanfang Metro* [NM15043]

right-hand corner of the photograph. The photograph is literally packed with people to the point that the ground (water and sand) is almost impossible to detect. Such depictions may be viewed as the visual equivalent of the verbal set phrase in Mandarin Chinese of 'people mountain people sea' (人山人海) which signifies a packed crowd (Gao, 2018: 1). Likewise, in Example B in Figure 2.5, the high-angle long shot allows audiences to gauge the scale or scope of the crowds and traffic (extending beyond the image frame) making their way home for the holidays. Such compositions construe Superlativeness.

Consonance (20 per cent) is construed through the depiction of people wearing traditional Chinese ethnic costumes, as they participate in traditional dances and ceremonies. Negativity is construed largely in the *Nanfang Metro* data. The only instance in *People's Daily* shows a young man climbing on a sacred statue for a photo opportunity. For Chinese target audiences such behaviour would arguably be viewed as norm-breaking/aberrant and this photograph thus constructs Negativity. Deviant behaviour (jumping over barriers, squeezing into already packed train carriages) is also a theme in the photographs in *Nanfang Metro*, as is traffic chaos on the highways. One photograph shows a person suffering (collapsed on the floor at a railway station) and being attended to by authorities.

Another pattern observed in the photography used in the ChinaDay corpus does not directly concern the construction of news values, but does explain the consistency of news values construction across the two years of data collected from *People's Daily*. In both 2015 and 2016, this news outlet published very similar photographs on what appear to be set themes: for example, school children's national day posters, travelling home by train, welcoming new babies born during the Golden Week, and various official/political ceremonies (see Figure 2.6). While not totally identical (but almost!) in their compositions, they are very similar in the meanings they construe, which suggests that the construction of news values from year to year is very similar. The photographs

Figure 2.6A Similarity in image capture in *People's Daily* across the years 2015 and 2016. PHOTOS: Left to right, top to bottom: PP15009, PP16016, PP15029, PP16022, PP15045_1, PP16034_2

published in *Nanfang Metro* are much more varied, although they too adhere to some of the same stock national day themes. Of particular interest in the photographs presented in Figure 2.6 (B) is the fact that the official photographs of the political elite are virtually identical. They are taken from the same angle, at the same moment in the activity sequence, and involving the same news actors. This means that the observation made in Section 2.1 in relation to the exact replication of verbal clauses year-on-year in *People's Daily* reporting of the national day also applies to the visual composition. Such levels of control over both verbal and visual content are 'admirable'. Ethnographic analysis would be necessary to provide information about how such similarities of composition come about (e.g. whether it is the photographer's decision or a directive).

Figure 2.6B Similarity in image capture in *People's Daily* across the years 2015 and 2016. PHOTOS: Left to right, top to bottom: PP15014_1, PP16012_2, PP15016, PP16011

In summing up the visual DNVA of the ChinaDay corpus, it is worth noting that different approaches to the discussion of the results may mask interesting differences in the visual styles of different news organisations. Aggregation of the results of visual DNVA indicates which news values are mainly constructed in relation to a particular topic. For example, in the reporting on the Chinese national day in two Chinese language news outlets, Proximity dominates, and Personalisation, Positivity and Eliteness are also construed. Such results suggest that the most visually newsworthy aspects of the Chinese national day are Chinese nationals, from both elite and everyday circles, participating in positive activities to do with nation building. However, there are interesting trends to be observed in the co-patterning of news values across these two news organisations. The photography used in *Nanfang Metro* focuses very much on the masses and the problems associated with the movement of so many people during the holiday, resulting in the co-patterning of Superlativeness with

Negativity and very little Personalisation. Almost the opposite is true of the construction of newsworthiness in the photographs used in *People's Daily*. This news organisation photographed individuals/family groups mostly being assisted or engaging in positive behaviours, resulting in a co-patterning of Personalisation with Positivity and virtually no Negativity. Looking at the collected data from these different perspectives sheds more light on how the Chinese national day was constructed in very different ways. It also sheds light on the potential influence of the levels of control and commercialisation on these two newspapers, as outlined in Section 1.3. *People's Daily* is the official newspaper of the CCP. Thus, one would expect very high levels of control over content, which is likely to reflect very positively on the government. *Nanfang Metro* belongs to a more commercialised branch of the state media, which is said to include more critical coverage of governments and Chinese society than in the past (Shi-xu, 2014: 120).

One final observation on the visual DNVA is that a qualified argument could well be made for the general applicability of the visual resources for newsworthiness construction beyond 'Western', English-language news outlets. In the majority of cases, the same visual resources tend to construe the same news values in the Chinese news photographs. Key differences exist in relation to measuring scope and scale and in the markers of elite status – for example, to what extent do any/all uniforms construe Eliteness? Discussions with Huan and other Chinese nationals suggest that not all uniforms construe Eliteness, since they are ubiquitous in China, from street cleaners and civil servants through to the highest military and political authorities. Thus, contextual cues (the type and rank of authority depicted) need to be taken into consideration when coding for Eliteness. Scope and scale also need to be measured in relation to norms that would be experienced on a daily basis by the target audiences of the news outlets. Research examining a range of news events, not just one topic, would also assist in uncovering additional resources that may be put to use in constructing newsworthiness. Finally, visual DNVA across a number of different cultural and linguistic contexts would help to determine which of the visual resources are truly universal.

2.3 Conclusion

News values analysis of the ChinaDay corpus demonstrates that the national day is constructed largely as a national commemoration involving the political elites. The reporting draws only very infrequently on the personal experiences of ordinary citizens and how they celebrate the national day. China and its political elites remain the focus of attention in national day reporting and are predominantly portrayed in a very positive light. The focus on Positivity in the Chinese data is in line with ben-Aaron's findings for older data from the United States (Independence Day), while Eliteness was only 'sometimes' found in her data (ben-Aaron, 2003: 95). The shared reporting in the ChinaDay corpus also includes references to commemorations that were held in Hong Kong, Macau and Tibet, thus bringing these sensitive territories under the same umbrella of nationhood.

In sum, the results of our analysis of the Chinese national day reporting are in line with ben-Aaron's (2003: 77) assessment of national holidays as a manifest-ation of 'applied nationalism' and Ting's (2017) reference to the role of national day reporting for the promotion of patriotism. In China's case, this is very much directed towards the promotion of national unity, national pride and conformity. However, we also found that another focus of attention was on tourism and entertainment, and the economic benefits from holiday travel. Thus, the com-mercialised aspects of the national day were also emphasised (in the verbal text).

In the next section, we examine the construction of newsworthiness in relation to another national day – Australia's national day. We do this to demonstrate the context-dependence of newsworthiness construction. What we find for a particular country's national day cannot be predicted to hold for another country. Thus, we would expect there to be differ-ences in the news values that are established in the Australian data, but given the importance of national days for 'applied nationalism' we would also expect certain similarities in the promotion of national unity. While the next section will mainly focus on describing the results for the Australian newspapers, the final section will provide a synthesis of results and comparison with the Chinese data.

3 Australia Day: A Conflicted Day of 'Celebration'

3.1 Using Corpus Linguistics to Analyse the AusDay Corpus

Our second study focuses on the Australian national day, officially known as *Australia Day*. As noted in Section 1, recent years have seen an increase in discussion about what it means to be Australian and how to acknowledge the history of this nation. Part of this discussion has focused on Australia Day itself, in particular on the date on which the public holiday falls. We can observe a discursive struggle in society, where alternative labels such as *Invasion Day* or *Survival Day* are used for this conflicted day of 'celebration' (NITV, 2017). The analysis presented in this section reveals how this discursive struggle is linguistically and visually reflected in the news values constructed in the reporting of the public holiday. Like Section 2, this section combines corpus-based discourse analysis of the verbal news reporting with analysis of visual resources. The analysis is, therefore, also an example of corpus-assisted multi-modal discourse analysis (CAMDA).

The section starts by examining the verbal component to uncover the linguistic construction of news values. We use collocation analysis (see Section 1) to uncover the range of labels used to name the national holiday as well as their frequency and distribution in the AusDay corpus. This reveals the extent to which the discursive struggle and the controversies around the day are included in the reporting by the news media. Having identified these labels, we then proceed to qualitative examination of each label within its context, via concordance analysis of full sentences. Qualitative analysis of the visual news reporting is presented in the second half of the section. Each photograph is analysed for the discursive construal of news values through close examination of its content (what is going on in the photograph) and of its capture (the composition and technical aspects of image recording).

3.1.1 General Observations

Before interrogating the AusDay corpus for the construction of newsworthiness, we first confirmed that the focus of the texts in our corpus is indeed on Australia Day. As a brief reminder here, we did **not** use a list of seed words to create our corpus (see Section 1). The word frequency list shows that the three most frequent non-grammatical word forms in the AusDay corpus are *Australia* (#1), *said* (#2) and *day* (#3).[15] The high frequency of *said* is common to corpora of news reporting, while the high frequency of *Australia* and *day* adequately reflects the focus on Australia Day.

Further, knowing that several alternative labels for this national day exist, we wanted to discover whether these alternatives occur in our corpus, how frequently they occur, and how they are distributed. To find out, we undertook a collocation analysis of the word *day* using Lancsbox/GraphColl (Brezina et al., 2015). The resulting GraphColl visualisation is shown in Figure 3.1, where shorter lines indicate a stronger association between words, as determined by the collocation measure MI3.[16] The visualisation only shows L1 collocates with an MI3 value of at least 7, and a minimum collocation frequency of 2.

---

[15] The word frequency list of the AusDay corpus is provided in Appendix 3 in the online appendices, www.cambridge.org/9781108814072.

[16] We use the MI3 measure (Daille, 1995), which is the cubed variant of the mutual information statistic, which reduces its low frequency bias; it gives more weight to observed frequencies, and ranks frequently occurring (typical) collocations much higher than those that are uncommon

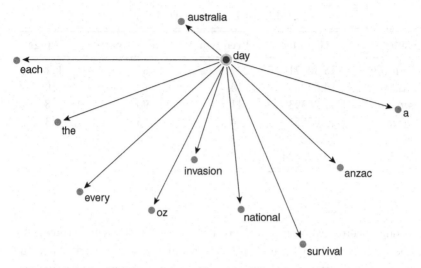

Figure 3.1 Visualisation of the collocates of *day* (L1, MI3 7.0, min. freq 2)

The GraphColl visualisation reveals that alternative labels for Australia Day are indeed used in Australian news reporting: *Australia Day, Oz Day, Invasion Day, national day* and *Survival Day*. However, Table 3.1 shows that there is a vast difference in how often these alternative labels occur and across how many texts. The columns in Table 3.1 provide information on the output from the collocation measure (the higher, the stronger the association), the frequency with which the word co-occurs with *day*, the frequency of the word in total, and the range (calculated separately through WordSmith since it is not provided in the GraphColl results). *Australia* and *day* are the most strongly associated, and the expression *Australia Day* has the highest frequency (247 instances) and widest range (111 out of 136 texts, or 82 per cent of the corpus). Alternative referring expressions have much lower frequencies in the two newspapers and occur in very few texts (between 1 and 10). *Invasion Day* and *national day* are the most frequent among the other labels for the national day (*Anzac Day* refers to a different public holiday in Australia). In sum, it is clear that *Australia Day* is the common, sanctioned term.

In terms of newsworthiness, both *Australia Day* and each of the alternative labels establish the news value of Timeliness, by referencing the day in articles that were published on or close to the actual day (see Section 1).

(Brezina et al., 2015: 159–60). While we use the GraphColl visualisation here to show the collocates of a single word (in essence, presenting some of the information in Table 3.1 in an alternative visual form), the program can also show collocation networks, illustrating the complex and multiple links between words.

Table 3.1 L1 collocates of *day*

Collocate	MI3 value	Freq (coll.)	Freq (corpus)	Range
australia	23.30671	247	483	111
invasion	14.62963	14	18	10
national	11.26393	11	90	8
anzac	11.05556	4	5	3
oz	10.13237	3	4	3
survival	7.792524	2	6	1

In other words, we argue that any reference to this event, whatever the label, will establish Timeliness for the Australian target audience. Since the design of our dataset used time as a variable (collecting articles within a one-week span of the national day), and since each label therefore automatically constructs Timeliness, we do not analyse the corpus any further for this news value.

In addition to Timeliness, it could be argued that the labels *national day, Oz Day,* and *Australia Day* establish Proximity for the audience by virtue of explicit reference to the target audience's community (the nation/ Australia). Further, the labels *Invasion Day* and *Survival Day* establish Negativity by pointing to the negative aspects around this public holiday, being associated with conflict and debate. It is questionable whether these labels also directly establish Proximity, as there is no explicit reference to Australia/the nation. However, cultural Proximity is indirectly constructed by these labels, as they refer to a conflict that is specific to contemporary Australian culture and would be familiar to the readers of *The Australian* and *The Sydney Morning Herald*.

In order to scrutinise further how the 'day' is constructed as newsworthy and given the low frequency of the non-grammatical collocates for *day* (except for *Australia*; see Table 3.1), we undertook qualitative concordance analysis. We used the WordSmith concordancer tool to carry out discursive news values analysis of each label in its co-text. Our unit of analysis, or span of co-text, was the sentence, although we expanded the co-text where necessary to unpack anaphoric references and the like. We start with the most frequent label *Australia Day* (Section 3.1.2). The less frequent alternative labels identified previously are discussed in Section 3.1.3. Note that the news values that are encapsulated in the labels themselves were not counted in the quantification of results.

3.1.2 Australia Day

Since the label *Australia Day* occurs most frequently in the AusDay corpus, we begin by examining patterns in the construction of newsworthiness in relation to this label.[17]

Concordance Analysis

Sorting the concordance lines for *Australia Day* alphabetically to the right identi-fied a number of recurring phrases that refer to an organisation (*Australia Day Council (Board)* [20 occurrences]) or to sub-events of the public holiday (e.g. *Australia Day honour/honours* [55 occurrences], *Australia Day address* [11 occur-rences], *a/an . . . Australia Day event/s* (5 occurrences), *Australia Day celebrations* [4 occurrences], *Australia Day awards* (4 occurrences), *Australia Day fireworks* [3 occurrences], *Australia Day billboard* (an advertisement featuring Muslim girls; 3 occurrences), and *Australia Day parade* [2 occurrences]). A selection of these phrases is displayed in Figure 3.2 (excluding *Australia Day Council [Board]* and *Australia Day honour/honours*).

Of these, *Australia Day Council (Board)* is a role label which establishes Eliteness, and we would also expect this news value to be constructed in the co-text of *Australia Day address,* since this speech features 'distinguished' community members:

> January 26 is a time to celebrate and reflect on our national spirit, and the Australia Day Address serves to focus our attention on what that means to all of us. Since 1997 the Address has drawn on distinguished members from within the community to express their unique perspective on our nation's identity and the diversity of our society.
>
> Each year the speaker is encouraged to share their experiences and reflect upon our history and our future, securing the Address as one of the most important Australia Day initiatives.
>
> (www.australiaday.com.au/events/australia-day-address/, accessed 20 March 2017)

Indeed, this is certainly the case with references to elite news actors such as, for example, politicians *Bill Shorten, Malcolm Turnbull, Mike Baird*; the use of adjectives and role labels (*renowned quantum physicist; NSW Premier; Professor*); and references to elite institutions (*American Australian Society*) also constructing Eliteness. However, concordance lines show that in the co-text of *Australia Day address*, Negativity, in

---

[17] When undertaking a concordance analysis, WordSmith retrieves 249 instances of *Australia Day* (across 111 texts) rather than the 247 listed in Table 3.1, since it processes the text differently (included are one instance of *anti-Australia day* and one instance of *Australia Day's*; see Appendix 4 online, www.cambridge.org/9781108814072).

26 at home in wintry Massachusetts, and giving the **Australia Day** address **at** the American Australian
, were as vivid as they were salutary. This year's **Australia Day** Address **celebrated** the immense and
quantum physicist Michelle Simmons for using her **Australia Day** address **earlier** this week to attack
quantum physicist Michelle Simmons used an **Australia Day** address **in** Sydney yesterday to warn
of state by 2020. Mr Shorten is expected to use his **Australia Day** address **in** Melbourne on Tuesday to
of the HSC physics curriculum. Delivering the 2017 **Australia Day** address **on** Tuesday, Professor
attempt to attract more girls to the subject. In her **Australia Day** address **on** Tuesday, quantum
Her big brother Gary went to the United States. In her **Australia Day** Address **on** Tuesday, she said she often
to Malcolm Turnbull's republican instincts in his **Australia Day** address, **saying** there is a unique
DAY NSW Premier Mike Baird has used his **Australia Day** address **to** warn that Australia is at risk
who immigrated to Australia in his teens, gave an **Australia Day** address **to** the Sydney Conservatorium

has called for greater transparency when awarding **Australia Day** awards **after** a transgender military
and charges of political correctness in the way the **Australia Day** awards **are** run and won, Mr Lasek said
scrutiny of the probity of the judging process for the **Australia Day** awards **as** it defends itself against
Australia Day awards **fallout** Canberra, that's in

Immigration Minister Peter Dutton has praised an **Australia Day** billboard **featuring** two Muslim
'I think it's great': Peter Dutton praises **Australia Day** billboard **featuring** Muslim girls
More than $100,000 raised to reinstate **Australia Day** billboard **with** Muslim girls, but not all

, celebrities and tourists - has closed its doors for **Australia Day** celebrations **because** of excessive
with indigenous Australians unhappy with the annual **Australia Day** celebrations **by** incorrectly using the
Star Observer, as the nation went back to work after **Australia Day** celebrations. **"He's** on a steep learning
simulating a lewd act with a dog during drunken **Australia Day** celebrations. The NRL has demanded
appeared on the Melbourne billboard was taken at an **Australia Day** event **in** the Docklands area last year,
. The billboard, promoting a government-funded **Australia Day** event **in** Melbourne, was
campaign was started after a billboard advertising an **Australia Day** event **in** Melbourne was removed due
been more consultation about the decision to cancel **Australia Day** events **in** Fremantle.'I would have
, which for the first time were a focal point of **Australia Day** events. **"There's** no difference
late yesterday, forcing the cancellation of the city's **Australia Day** fireworks **for** the first time in the
ignore veto Business owners have reinstated **Australia Day** fireworks **in** the West Australian port
last August that it would cancel its annual **Australia Day** fireworks, **preferring** instead to host a
focus was on kicking back. Like the nation itself, the **Australia Day** parade **in** Melbourne was a diverse mix
in Adelaide's CBD last night with a 4000-strong **Australia Day** parade **representing** groups from 100

Figure 3.2 A selection of recurring phrases starting with *Australia Day*

the form of opposition, is also constructed in the phrases *warn against the dumbing down of; a "disaster"; criticising; warn that Australia is at risk of losing its character to anti-immigration politics.* The construction of Positivity is very limited, but can be seen in the following example (EX1 – marked in bold), which celebrates Australia as a country to offer freedom and refuge to immigrants:

EX 1.　This year's Australia Day Address **celebrated the immense and prized free-dom** that the young Australian, who arrived in Sydney as a refugee in 1998, will never take for granted. S16004[18]

One specific aspect of the Australia Day celebrations concerns the Australia Day honours – the official awards given to people who have made an outstanding contribution to Australian society. The construction of Positivity is encapsulated in the nominal group *Australia Day honour/honours* itself, but it is also repeated in the cited responses of recipients on receiving the award (*wonderful feeling and it is*

---

[18]　The ID numbers listed next to the examples indicate which newspaper they are from [S=*Sydney Morning Herald*; A=*The Australian*], the year of publication [16=2016; 17=2017] and the text number, e.g. 004.

a genuine privilege). However, once again the Positivity one might expect to be associated with these awards is overshadowed by the construction of Negativity. Thus, the nominal group *Australia Day awards* is used in the co-text of references to controversies in how the recipients of awards are chosen, which construct Negativity (*charges of being overtly politically correct, progressive and cause-driven, instead of merit-based; fallout; called for greater transparency when awarding; the current controversy and charges of political correctness*).

Ben-Aaron (2003: 77–8) notes that 'national holiday celebrations are manifested materially as sets of ceremonial practices such as flag displays and ceremonies, parades, bell ringing, fireworks'. Thus, nominal phrases such as *Australia Day fireworks/parade/celebrations* would be likely to construct Australia Day as something that is celebrated, and hence should point to the news value of Positivity. In this dataset, however, this is not the case. For example, the phrase *Australia Day fireworks* refers to an accident that led to the cancellation of the fireworks (EX2) and a controversy over attempts to move celebrations to a different date (EX3), thus construing Negativity. Unexpectedness (unusuality) and Superlativeness (amount of people) are also constructed in EX2 in *for the first time in the 32-year history of an event that was expected to attract 300,000 people.*

EX 2. **Two people were killed** when a seaplane plunged into Perth's Swan River late yesterday, **forcing the cancellation** of the city's Australia Day fireworks for the first time in the 32-year history of an event that was expected to attract 300,000 people. A17020

EX 3. Business owners have reinstated Australia Day fireworks in the West Australian port city of Fremantle, where the local council **caused a furore by attempting to move all the usual public holiday events to January 28**. Fremantle council announced last August that **it would cancel its annual Australia Day fireworks**, preferring instead to host a free music festival tomorrow, "a culturally inclusive alternative event" called One Day. A17027

Likewise, all instances of *Australia Day celebrations* refer to negative happenings, for example, disruption of the moral order through bad behaviour (EX4), disagreement (EX5), negative action (EX6), and a linguistic error (EX7), pointing to a key difference in the construction of newsworthiness around the Australian national day 'celebrations' compared with ben-Aaron's (2003) analysis of the US national day, July Fourth (see Section 1).

EX 4. Mitchell Pearce's NRL **career could be over** after the Roosters captain was filmed **simulating a lewd act with a dog during drunken Australia Day celebrations**. S16048

EX 5. **A rift between** RAAF reservist Group Captain McGregor [Queensland's nominee for Aus of the Year] and her former boss, retired Lieutenant General

Morrison [Australian of the Year as announced on Aus Day], the former chief of the army, was aired in a gay and lesbian journal, the Star Observer, as the nation went back to work after Australia Day celebrations. A16029

EX 6. One of Adelaide's top restaurants – popular with politicians, celebrities and tourists – has **closed its doors** for Australia Day celebrations **because of excessive penalty rates**. A16026

EX 7. He [Bill Shorten] also had **an unfortunate slip-up** when he was sympathising with indigenous Australians unhappy with the annual Australia Day celebrations **by incorrectly using the word "disposition"**. A16024

Finally, co-textual analysis of *Australia Day billboard* and *a/an ... Australia Day event/s* shows that occurrences have a low range, and that both Negativity and Positivity are constructed. For example, a billboard that showed Muslim Australian girls in hijabs is referenced in relation to both praise and controversy (see further 'Collocation Analysis' below).

Together, the recurring phrases just analysed make up 107 of the 249 instances of *Australia Day*. Among the remaining 142 instances, *Australia Day* is also occasionally used preceding nouns or noun phrases (37 instances), pointing to the different topics that are reported on in relation to the public holiday:

> *2017 honours list, ambassadors, **anarchy**, appointment, avowal, **bender**, biscuit, blue cap, break, citizenship ceremony, cockroach race event, commemorations, concert, crowd, doodles, gong, google drawing, holiday, lamb ad, **march**, message, organisation, panel, party, press conference, promotion, **protesters**, **protests**, public holiday, revellers, **ruckus**, **scandal**, sign, speaker, speech, weekend.*

With the exception of *Australia Day crowd* (which occurs twice), all occur only once in the AusDay corpus, although some of these words are partial synonyms to words already discussed above (e.g. *speech – address; gong – award*). Several indicate the likely presence of Negativity (marked in bold), but to confirm that this is the case it is necessary to fully analyse the sentences in which these and the other remaining instances occur.

Figure 3.3 summarises the construction of news values in relation to *Australia Day* in these 142 instances (in percentages). In the analysis, the construction of each news value was only counted once per sentence, even if the same news value was constructed by more than one linguistic device. If the same sentence established two or more different news values, it was analysed as constructing all of these values. Hence, results do not add up to 100 per cent in total. Thus, a percentage value of 60 per cent simply indicates that this particular news value was established in 60 per cent of analysed sentences.

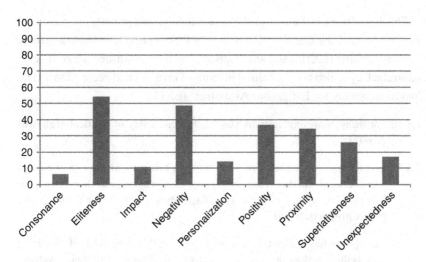

Figure 3.3 The construction of news values in relation to *Australia Day* (in percentages)

The most frequently constructed news value is Eliteness (54 per cent). This news value is established through the use of specific role labels (*Federal Greens leader, Queensland Premier, former prime minister, Aboriginal Elder, a marquee player for the Sydney Roosters*) and proper names (*Julia Gillard, Linda Burney, Gladys Berejiklian*), and very often these are combined (*Kon Karapanagiotidis, CEO of the Asylum Seeker Resource Centre*). There are very few instances of generic role labels such as *leaders, ambassadors, dignitaries*. Eliteness tends to co-occur with Negativity, as elite news actors are cited in comments on the emerging discourses of struggle in relation to Australia Day, as demonstrated in examples 8 and 9, where elite news actors (underlined) are cited on the debate surrounding the 'change the date' campaign:

EX 8. Deputy Prime Minister Barnaby Joyce has **lashed out** at people who want to change the date of Australia Day, labelling them **"miserable gutted"** and arguing the idea was **"political correctness gone mad"**. S17013

EX 9. Having said on Wednesday that he would be celebrating Australia Day on January 26, Bill Shorten yesterday **acknowledged controversy over the date** in a speech at a citizenship ceremony in his electorate. A17023

In fact, Negativity (49 per cent) seems to be more important as a news value than Positivity (37 per cent). Bednarek and Caple (2017: 60–1) note that it may be useful to further distinguish what type of Negativity is established (e.g. accidents vs. opposition/division vs. terrorism vs. crime). In the AusDay corpus, Negativity is constructed in relation to different events, including political crisis, civil unrest and an accident that occurred on the day.

The first of these is the change-the-date campaign and protests that took place in cities around the country. References to these events construct the day as political conflict (EX10), and as an opportunity for civil disobedience (EX11). Australia Day is also contextualised in terms of invasion and occupation and the loss of autonomy for Indigenous Australians (EX12).

EX 10. For many, however, Australia Day has become **a day of political argument**. A16023

EX 11. Left Renewal, which has **vowed to "fight to bring about the end of capital-ism", caused further controversy by encouraging members** and other Australia Day protesters **to burn the flag, interrupt celebrations and graffiti public property**. S17017

EX 12. They [protesters] called for the date of Australia Day to be changed, as January 26 was **the day their land was invaded, the "beginning of all their troubles"**. S17012

As already seen in the analysis of *Australia Day awards*, Negativity is also constructed in relation to events concerning these awards. News articles report the criticism that was levelled at the awards panel for being shrouded in secrecy (EX13), and at the nominations process for the underrepresentation of female nominees (EX14). Newspapers also reported Children's Laureate and author Jackie French's feeling of guilt for receiving an award that favours eloquent and high-profile Australians, while ignoring the thousands working much harder to improve children's literacy (EX15).

EX 13. Australia Day panel **like a 'papal conclave'** A16030

EX 14. This Australia Day, **seven of the 31 categories had no female nominations**. S16021

EX 15. For Jackie French, the thrill of receiving a gong on Australia Day is **tinged with guilt**. S16027

Negativity also often combines with the news value of Impact,[19] and in this dataset, both are construed in relation to workplace issues. Four stories include criticisms of employees who take sick leave around Australia Day, rather than applying for annual leave (EX16), while employers are described as closing on Australia Day because of the costs involved in paying employees public holiday

---

[19] It is difficult to assess whether Impact should include references to significant effects/conse-quences that are limited to particular individuals. In a previous project, we did not categorise items as constructing Impact if the reported event explicitly affects only a few people (Bednarek, 2016b). Here, we decided to use a less strict categorisation of Impact, as evident from the examples.

penalty rates (EX17). In another story, Negativity is construed in relation to the actions of a small business owner, who is referenced as referring to Australia Day using negative evaluative language as *national dickhead day* on signage outside his café (EX18). The vandalism and threats he received as a consequence are also reported (Impact).

EX 16. Australia Day falls on a Tuesday this year and **bosses are already bracing themselves for an influx of people calling in sick** on Monday to score themselves a four-day weekend. S16003

EX 17. Yesterday, on the restaurant's front window, was a message to patrons that said: "Parlamento will be **closed** on Australia Day **due to public holiday costs.**" A16026

EX 18. The owner of Mister Jones in Bermagui said his business has been **targeted by vandals** and his **voicemail flooded with threats** after a local man photographed the sign "Yes, we're open on **national dickhead day**" – a reference to them being open for business on Australia Day, January 26 – and uploaded it to Facebook on Monday. S16049

Finally, Negativity and Impact are established in EX19 through negative lexis (*plunged into river … killing*) in referring to a very public accident that occurred on Australia Day, when a sea plane crashed into the Swan River, in Perth, Western Australia:

EX 19. Mining executive and father of three Peter Lynch appeared to have been attempting to accelerate out of a turn that had become a steep bank when his **vintage seaplane plunged into Perth's Swan River, instantly killing him and his partner** in front of an Australia Day crowd of 60,000. A17030

Being able to tease out and group the different types of Negativity construed in relation to an event allows researchers to engage in more nuanced discussion of the newsworthy aspects of that event. In the AusDay corpus, Negativity is construed in relation to political conflict, workplace issues, and accidental death. Identifying sub-categories such as these further demonstrates how news values tend to co-occur.

As is already evident, Australian news media do engage in some discussion of the controversies around the national day, thus exposing the nation's face to scrutiny of how nationhood is constructed and remembered. Across the two years of data collection, there was a noticeable increase in the amount of political debate in 2017 compared to 2016. This reflects the growing momentum that this debate is now receiving in Australia (see Section 1). However, several stories do also construe the day as positive, focusing in particular on reconciliation (EX20) and multiculturalism (EX21).

EX 20. Canberra teenager Ineka Voigt **wants to see a "message of reconciliation" continue to spread** after an enormous response from the public to her Australia Day Google drawing. S16045

EX 21. Noel Pearson says Australia Day should be **a day to celebrate our Indigenous heritage, our British inheritance and our multicultural achievement**, she [Shireen Morris, advisor to Noel Pearson on constitutional recognition] said. S16009

In addition, Positivity is construed in relation to the Australia Day awards, principally through direct quotation of statements made by the recipients, reflecting on the honour this award bestows on them (EXs 22 and 23). This also occurs in the co-text of the recurring phrase *Australia Day honour(s)*, as already mentioned.

EX 22. Of his [Captain Richard de Crespigny, pilot] Australia Day appointment he says: "This was **the most wonderful surprise** and I am **very honoured** to get it." S16038

EX 23. I'm **absolutely delighted and very appreciative of an honour of this nature** on Australia Day, Ms Gillard tells Fairfax Media before departing for Africa. S17010

The taking up of Australian citizenship, a tradition performed on Australia Day, is also largely construed positively (EX24), through the reference to the new citizens' positive emotion, *their love of/for* (foregrounded through repetition and parallelism).

EX 24. **Their love of science inspired them to move here, their love for each other drew them into a relationship and their love for this country inspired them to become citizens together** on Australia Day. A17022

Proximity is established through references to place names (*Redfern, Sydney, Willoughby*) and to Aboriginal Australians (*Aboriginal Australians, Aboriginal elder*). A small number of articles also make use of the local vernacular *Aussie* and *mate* (EX 25), both of which are iconic words of Australian English. These are examples of how the use of a particular dialect can construct Proximity (Bednarek & Caple, 2017: 92).

EX 25. This is Australia Day and if you don't like it, I don't know **mate**, go to work, do something else. S17013

Quite surprisingly, Personalisation is construed in only 13 instances in this dataset. Celebrations of Australia Day are viewed as an opportunity for families and friends to get together around the barbecue to celebrate (also reflected in advertising campaigns[20]) and one would expect that there would be ample

---

[20] In 2017, Meat & Livestock Australia produced the following ad, centered on the barbecue: https://www.youtube.com/watch?v=fBTWc4i_Fhw.

opportunity to report on such celebrations. In this dataset, however, Personalisation is construed quite specifically in relation to migrants (EX26) and Indigenous Australians (EX27).

EX 26. **Mr Khan**'s [Pakistani asylum seeker] Australia Day, surrounded by hundreds of like-minded people, was in stark contrast to how he used to celebrate Pakistan's Independence Day on August 14 with friends and family. A16027

EX 27. **Alice Springs woman Jacinta Nampijimpa Price** says she was so outraged on Australia Day when she saw on television a campaign sign reading "change the date – smash the state" that she sat down and turned on her computer. A17031

It could be argued that the various references to immigration and multicultural-ism (see also examples 1, 21 and 24) aim to construct national unity and a sense of pride in such multicultural nationhood in Australia.

Collocation Analysis

The results so far come from the qualitative analysis of concordance lines, and it is not clear whether a different corpus linguistic technique would have uncovered the same findings. As it is important to triangulate techniques in corpus linguistics (see e.g. Marchi & Taylor, 2009, Baker & Egbert, 2016), we therefore also undertook a brief collocation analysis of *Australia Day*.[21] We identified collocates of *Australia Day* in a window of five words on either side (5:5), with a minimum MI-score of 3, a minimum collocate frequency of 4, and a minimum log likelihood value of 4 (where an LL value of 3.84 corresponds to $p < 0.05$). Combining the two metrics (MI and LL) allows one 'to extract collocations that are both lexically interesting and statistically significant' (Baker et al., 2013: 37). With these restrictions, thirty-four collocates are found, with a range of between two and forty-nine texts.[22] Such a collocation analysis would have given us some pointers to potential news values constructed in the corpus, such as:

- Eliteness (*OAM, AC, AO, AM, Gillard, council, board, leaders, Simmons*)[23]
- Positivity (*honours, honour, celebrations, celebrated, awards*)

---

[21] WordSmith settings: WordList: hyphens not allowed in words; ' not allowed within word; Collocate settings: L5:R5, stop at sentence break, min. freq. 2, min. length 1, min. texts 1, separate search-words, not case-sensitive. Further restrictions imposed via Excel filtering of results.

[22] The distribution across texts is as follows: 2 collocates in 2 texts; 4 collocates in 3 texts; 7 in 4; 3 in 5; 4 in 6; 3 in 7; 2 in 9; 2 in 10; and one collocate each in 11, 12, 30, 31, 32, 41 and 49 texts. The most distributed collocates are *honours* (49 texts); # (41 texts); *to* (32 texts), *on* (31 texts), and *a* (30 texts).

[23] The acronyms *OAM, AC, AO, AM* stand for different levels of the Order of Australia: Medal (OAM), Companion (AC), Officer (AO), and Member (AM).

1 exist within the Greens. Mr Shoebridge addressed the invasion day rally, demanding the date of Australia Day be changed. Rising tensions spilled into the open on Friday, with Greens elder Bob
2 conservative, Anglo-Celtic Australian, I want to play a part in the push to changing the date of Australia Day. I believe it is an important issue, and to prevent a potential schism in Australia's society
3 Deputy Prime Minister Barnaby Joyce has lashed out at people who want to change the date of Australia Day, labelling them "miserable gutted" and arguing the idea was "political correctness
4 day" rallies chanted "always was, always will be Aboriginal land". They called for the date of Australia Day to be changed, as January 26 was the day their land was invaded, the "beginning
5 devastating effects on Indigenous people and culture. On the matter of changing the date of Australia Day, Ms Voigt said she was undecided, but she hoped to see continuing change in the
6 in a speech at a citizenship ceremony in his electorate. "Whatever one's view about the date of Australia Day, I think we can all agree that we should remember our first Australians, for whom
7 and more profound issues, including constitutional recognition, to deal with than the date of Australia Day." Having said on Wednesday that he would be celebrating Australia Day on
8 issued like constitutional recognition (for indigenous Australians) to deal with than the date of Australia Day," he said. One Nation leader Pauline Hanson, who used social media to call for

Figure 3.4 'Australia Day' with context word *date* (L5:R5)

1 maintained. "Everyone is entitled to a point of view but I think most Australians accept January 26 as Australia Day," the Prime Minister said. "It is a day where we celebrate the rich diversity of all
2 on January 26; first official "Invasion Day" marked in Sydney 1994: January 26 formally becomes Australia Day.
3 , to deal with than the date of Australia Day." Having said on Wednesday that he would be celebrating Australia Day on January 26. Bill Shorten yesterday acknowledged controversy over the date
4 "invasion day" rallies chanted "always was, always will be Aboriginal land". They called for the date of Australia Day to be changed, as January 26 was the day their land was invaded, the "beginnin
5 doesn't resolve much of the very valid national debate that needs to be had about the celebration of Australia Day on January 26th.'
6 the sign "Yes, we're open on national dickhead day" - a reference to them being open for business on Australia Day, January 26 - and uploaded it to Facebook on Monday. The photo was then she
7 Call to rethink national celebration in interests of mutual recognition AUSTRALIA DAY For many Australians, January 26 will be marked by beers, barbecues and A
8 Arts Centre, Ms Berejiklian said there were more appropriate days to debate the issue of whether Australia Day should be celebrated on January 28, and ways to demand change. "We have a c

Figure 3.5 'Australia Day' with context word *January* (L5:R5)

1 for racial and religious tolerance. The campaign was started after a billboard advertising an Australia Day event in Melbourne was removed due to social media outrage and threats
2 Day billboard featuring Muslim girls Immigration Minister Peter Dutton has praised an Australia Day billboard featuring two Muslim Australian girls in hijabs, and backed the
3 values." The photograph that appeared on the Melbourne billboard was taken at an Australia Day event in the Docklands area last year, and was part of a rotating series of in
4 the wearing of Islamic dress in public. The billboard, promoting a government-funded Australia Day event in Melbourne, was controversially taken down after threats were ma
5 'I think it's great': Peter Dutton praises Australia Day billboard featuring Muslim girls Immigration Minister Peter Dutton has pr
6 More than $100,000 raised to reinstate Australia Day billboard with Muslim girls, but not all are happy It took just a matter of h

Figure 3.6 'Australia Day' with context word *billboard* (L5:R5)

- Proximity (*national, Sydney, nation, Melbourne*)
- Timeliness (*Tuesday, yesterday*)

Additional collocates include *address*, *date*, *on*, *billboard*, *January*, # [numbers], *list*, *used*, *this*, *event*, *like*, *to*, *a*, and *its*, and allow us to identify some of the recurring phrases we mentioned above (*Australia Day address*, *Australia Day billboard*, *Australia Day event*), without pointing to specific news values. What is particularly surprising is that none of the collocates point directly to the news value of Negativity, which seems so dominant in the dataset. However, if we examine the use of the seemingly neutral collocates *date*, *January*, and *billboard* we are indeed able to identify this Negativity. Figure 3.4 shows how the newspapers reference the conflict about the date of Australia Day, in particular the desire (l. 1 *demanding*, l.2 *push*, l.3 *want to*, l. 4 *called for*, l. 8 *calling for*) to change the date.

Similarly, the occurrences of *January* as a collocate of *Australia Day* (Figure 3.5) reference the different viewpoints (l. 1), controversy (l. 3), or debate (l. 5, l. 8) about 26 January, and the calls to change or rethink the date (l. 4, 7).

The concordance lines for the collocate *billboard* (Figure 3.6) also show the construction of Negativity, this time in relation to racism/Islamophobia, social media outrage and *threats* (l. 1, 4), controversy (l. 4), and unhappiness (l. 6).

In other words, we can identify the presence of the news value of Negativity when we examine certain collocates in more detail, but the question is whether we would have chosen to analyse seemingly neutral words such as *date*,

January, and *billboard* if we had not already undertaken the concordance analysis and therefore knew what we were looking for. As we can see, quite a different picture of the data emerges if the starting point is collocation as opposed to concordance analysis. This is not surprising because the co-textual span is different, particular thresholds such as minimum frequency were applied, and because the collocation analysis relies on the repeated use of the same words in the immediate co-text of the label. In contrast, concordance analysis is not reliant on such automated pattern recognition. In addition, a concordance simply presents all instances of a search term, focussing on occurrence, whereas the collocation results are the basis of integrating statistical (word association) measures. One conclusion that we can draw from this triangulation is that where news values analysis is undertaken through colloca-tion analysis, the analysis should go beyond obvious 'pointers' to news values and should always involve follow-up analysis of full sentences.

In sum, the corpus-based discourse analysis so far suggests that the Australian news media reporting of Australia Day (and its associated events) does not align with ben-Aaron's suggestion that news reporting on national holidays is mostly a 'manifestation of politeness' (2003: 97). The face of the nation being exposed in the news reporting we investigated is one that is struggling with how to imagine itself and how to include all of the communities and their memories and stories. Negativity (in the form of controversy, conflict, debate) dominates. By exposing the criticisms, controversies and conflicts surrounding the national day, audiences are presented with the opportunity to question their own understandings of this holiday and how they will choose to remember it going forward. As Australian residents engaging regularly with the media, two of the authors have noticed that each year, dissenting voices are getting louder and louder and the news media cover these voices in their reporting. It is somewhat surprising that this is the case in the co-text of the 'neutral', frequent, and sanctioned term *Australia Day*. We would have mostly expected this to occur in references to the 'activist' labels *Invasion Day* and *Survival Day*, which point directly to the conflict/opposition. The co-text of these and the other alternative referring expressions is explored in the next section.

3.1.3 *Alternative Labels:* Invasion Day, Survival Day, national day, Oz Day

As noted in Section 3.1.1, while much less frequent than the use of the official label *Australia Day*, a number of other labels that refer to the national day are also used in reporting this event (*Invasion Day, Survival Day, national day, Oz Day*). This set of labels is also dominated by the news value of Negativity, although the Negativity is much more closely tied to the opposition to how the nation celebrates the day.

The label *Invasion Day* only occurs in 10 of the 136 articles in the AusDay corpus. As predicted, the Negativity constructed in the co-text of this label is mainly associated with opposition and division. This opposition is referenced through negative lexis such as *march* (EX28), *detractors* (EX29), *protesters* (EX32), *rallies* (EX34), and *demonstrators* (EX35). In several cases, the opposition and division seem to be constructed as condemnable, through descriptions of negative actions such as assaulting police, flag-burning and spray-painting. Example 33 explicitly emphasises the peaceful nature of most of the protests. Interestingly, there is no clear-cut distinction between the right-leaning *Australian* and the left-leaning *Sydney Morning Herald* here:

EX 28. 'Invasion Day' **suspect**; A man arrested for allegedly **assaulting police** during **the flag-burning melee** at the "invasion day" march. S17017

EX 29. Asked about **those who regarded the day as "Invasion Day"**, Mr Wilson said: "There'll always be **detractors**, but . . . ." A16023

EX 30. . . . some indigenous people **who identify January 26 [. . .] as "Invasion Day".** A17027

EX 31. . . . is **not embraced by** many Australians who call it "Invasion Day". S17013

EX 32. . . . the "invasion day" protesters who **burned the national flag and clashed with police** on Australia Day. S17012

EX 33. "Invasion Day" protests were held peacefully in Brisbane and Melbourne, while hundreds of people **staged a sit-in** outside Parliament House in Canberra. A17022

EX 34. **Protesters took to the streets** for "Invasion Day" rallies. A17023

EX 35. About 150 **demonstrators** swarmed central Melbourne chanting "no pride in genocide" while the words "Happy Invasion Day" were **spray-painted on a train station wall**. A16028

There are only two instances of *Survival Day* in the AusDay corpus, co-occurring with *Invasion Day* and appearing in one text (EX36). In this text, Negativity is construed more generally in relation to the rights of Aboriginal people in Australia both in the past and today, and pointing to the long history of protest led by Aboriginal and Torres Strait Islander people:

EX 36. 'Invasion day and **survival day**'
Kali Bellear, whose father Bob Bellear was deeply involved in the civil rights movement and then became the first Aboriginal judge, said growing up watching parents and uncles being arrested at protests "made me realise that Aboriginal people had to fight every step of the way for their rights . . . today is invasion day but also **survival day**". A17025

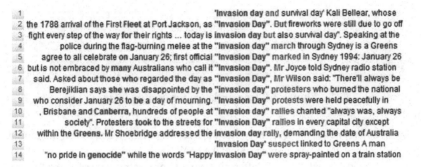

1 'Invasion day and survival day' Kali Bellear, whose
2 the 1788 arrival of the First Fleet at Port Jackson, as "Invasion Day". But fireworks were still due to go off
3 fight every step of the way for their rights ... today is invasion day but also survival day'. Speaking at the
4 police during the flag-burning melee at the "invasion day" march through Sydney is a Greens
5 agree to all celebrate on January 26; first official "Invasion Day" marked in Sydney 1994: January 26
6 but is not embraced by many Australians who call it "Invasion Day". Mr Joyce told Sydney radio station
7 said. Asked about those who regarded the day as "Invasion Day", Mr Wilson said: "There'll always be
8 Berejiklian says she was disappointed by the "invasion day" protesters who burned the national
9 who consider January 26 to be a day of mourning. "Invasion Day" protests were held peacefully in
10 , Brisbane and Canberra, hundreds of people at "invasion day" rallies chanted "always was, always
11 society". Protesters took to the streets for "Invasion Day" rallies in every capital city except
12 within the Greens. Mr Shoebridge addressed the invasion day rally, demanding the date of Australia
13 'Invasion Day' suspect linked to Greens A man
14 "no pride in genocide" while the words "Happy Invasion Day" were spray-painted on a train station

Figure 3.7 The use of quotation marks around *Invasion Day*

In example 36 (and in example 27), the reporting has included reference to and the voices of Aboriginal Australians. However, a previous study of the AusDay corpus showed that only a quarter of the texts appear to refer to Aboriginal or Torres Strait Islander people(s) or matters (Bednarek, Caple & Huan, in press). This shows that a sub-set of the reporting on Australia Day may refer to Indigenous people(s) or matters, but a majority appears to contain no such references. Further, both activist labels (*Survival Day*, *Invasion Day*) are almost always enclosed in quotation marks (EX36 and Figure 3.7).

In the context of news reporting, it is difficult to assess whether such quotation marks around words just indicate that the label is not the writer's own, or whether there is an explicit distancing from the label. The co-text can provide some clues, but how these quotation marks are read also depends on the reader's attitude (for further discussion, see Caple & Bednarek, in press). What we **can** say is that these labels are treated as labels used by others – unnamed Australians, protestors or Aboriginal and Torres Strait Islander people, although there are differences between texts in terms of the attitude that is implied towards these others as noted (e.g. ... *is not embraced by many Australians who call it "invasion day"* [EX31] vs *"invasion day" protesters who burned the national flag* [EX32]).

Finally, in relation to the other two alternative labels, *national day* and *Oz Day*, the news value of Negativity continues to dominate the construction of newsworthiness. For example, negative lexis and evaluative language are immediately apparent in the KWIC view of the concordance in lines 1–5 and 7–9 of Figure 3.8 (e.g. *attacks, gutted, critics, mourning, did not agree, protesters, killing, activists, could not be united, terrible wrongdoings, fraught topic, resistance*).

This Negativity is typically in the form of references to opposition/division, as examples 37 and 38 show in more detail:

1		Joyce attacks 'gutted' critics of national day Date debate: Former colleagues clash Deputy Prime Minister Barnaby Jo
2	but unlike NSW they mark it on the nearest Monday to create a long weekend 1938 First official "national day of mourning" marked by Aboriginal leaders 1988: States and territories
3	respect and inclusion when planning events to commemorate the nation's day. "For some our national day is associated with thoughts of mourning, struggle and survival," the me:
4	tapestry." The Prime Minister did not agree with calls to change the date of the country's national day from the anniversary of the landing of the First Fleet 229 years ago, out c
5	opposition to same-sex marriage. In Sydney, more than 1000 protesters marked Australia's national "day of killing" by marching from Redfern to Town Hall, where activists triec
6	industry, resources and science minister Ian Macfarlane, revealed his newfound belief that the national day should move "to remove a potential roadblock to reconciliation and a g
7	to reconciliation and a greater Australia." He said Australians could not be united around the national day because, to some, it represents "terrible wrongdoings". "It's about healir
8	should be able to express a view on the matter". A research fellow told The Australian the national day issue was a "fraught topic". "A lot of people have legitimate complaints
9	, candidates and political staffers, is trying to orchestrate a week-long "resistance" against the national day. Left Renewal has called on supporters to steal and burn the "Aus rag" -
10	inflicted his leadership a fatal blow by knighting Prince Philip, several premiers ushered in the national day by signing a document - prepared by the Australian Republican Movem
11	of Sydney's department of history, said the past 20 years has seen the day emerge as a "truly national day". He said a transition in the past two decades has transformed the day t

Figure 3.8 Concordance for *national day*

EX 37. Sydney newspaper The Daily Telegraph has reported that Left Renewal, a radical splinter group which sprang out of the NSW Greens and includes party members, candidates and political staffers, **is trying to orchestrate a week-long "resistance" against** the national day. A17001

EX 38. "For some our national day is associated with thoughts of **mourning, struggle and survival**," the message [by the Melbourne Institute for Indigenous Development] read. A17011

Even though they are relatively infrequent, it is safe to assume that both *Invasion Day* and *national day* have a negative semantic prosody in this dataset. We use the term *semantic prosody* (Louw, 1993) here to refer to what Bednarek (2008) calls *POS/NEG collocation* – the co-occurrence of a word with a set of words that are positive or negative. Such a co-occurrence pattern does not automatically indicate that the expressions have a negative connotation (think of the verb *heal*: for further discussion, see Bednarek, 2008).

Overall, there is very little Positivity constructed in relation to the alternative labels for Australia Day. In this final example (EX39), it could be argued that Positivity is established through the description of a positive action:

EX 39. The Greens-led council **made the decision out of respect for some indigenous people** who identify January 26, marking the 1788 arrival of the First Fleet at Port Jackson, as "Invasion Day". A17027

However, the assessment of Positivity in relation to this example is very dependent on the target audience. As Bednarek and Caple (2017: 61) note: 'certain target audiences might perceive a particular reported event as [positive], while others would not.' This article was published in *The Australian*, a newspaper that is well-known for its reporting of Indigenous issues, while distancing itself from Greens-led initiatives. Thus, there may be many readers who would not read this positively, and we would also have to analyse the wider co-text to see how readers are positioned. Also note the hedging use of *some* in example 39, which qualifies the number of Indigenous Australians who identify January 26 as Invasion Day. This final example reminds us that in order to minimise over-interpretation, DNVA must always take into consideration the target audience of the news outlets that are being investigated.

1	can understand that indigenous Australians don't see January 26 as a **day of celebration.** "For them, it was a day of disposition,'
2	don't see January 26 as a day of celebration. "For them, it was a **day of disposition,"** Mr Shorten said.
3	and the message that sends to Aboriginal Australians on what is a **day of grieving** and protest for them. Online: Human righ
4	he described it as "a very complex day". For most Australians, it was a **day of leisure.** In Sydney, Bernie and Jill Cook, with daugh
5	woman who is deputy leader of the Labor Party in NSW, it is a **day of mixed** emotions. She said Australia Day better refle
6	a rare Tuesday off work. For Indigenous Australians it will be a **day of mourning.** It marks the start of British invasion on
7	with indigenous Australians who consider January 26 to be a **day of mourning.** "Invasion Day" protests were held peace
8	be detractors, but like the vast majority of Australians, I think it's a **day of national** celebration." As to what it meant to be Au
9	how lucky we are." For many, however, Australia Day has become a **day of political** argument. The new Australian of the Year,

Figure 3.9 Concordance lines for *a day of*

3.1.4 A Day of Mourning

Finally, to check whether our analysis of the labels missed any additional references to the national day, we also examined a concordance of *day.*[24] We ignored instances of the labels we already analysed as well as unrelated occurrences such as *race day, a day at the races, half a day in court, all day, Cup day, each/every day, one day,* etc. Patterns that confirm the tendencies identified are evident both in post-modification and pre-modification of the noun. Thus, the co-text of the phrase *a day of* (shown in the KWIC view in Figure 3.9) most often also establishes the news value of Negativity since it includes negative lexis such as *political argument*, *mixed emotions*, *disposition* (a politician's slip of the tongue for *dispossession*), *mourning*, *grieving* and *protest.*

Even the two instances that co-occur with *celebration* (l. 1, 8.) point to arguments over the day when we expand the co-text:

EX 40. Asked about **those who regarded the day as "Invasion Day"**, Mr Wilson said: "There'll always be **detractors**, but **like the vast majority of Australians, I think it's a day of national celebration**." A16023

EX 41. "I can understand that **indigenous Australians don't see January 26 as a day of celebration**. For them, it was a day of disposition [dispossession]," Mr Shorten said. A16024

Examples such as these confirm the construction of Negativity in relation to this national holiday, regardless of how it is labelled. They reveal aspects of the discursive struggle associated with the day, with its timing and history, and point to emerging trends around the need for discussion and eventually for change. In

[24] Note that using frequency as a starting point (i.e. focussing on expressions that include *day*) misses an additional referring expression that is relatively infrequent in the corpus: *holiday.* However, only three of the twelve instances are both relevant and not already captured by analysing *Australia Day* (as it often occurs in the same sentence). For reference, two of these instances occur in headlines and construct Negativity by reference to (i) the rise in employees taking sick leave on the Friday following the Thursday public holiday, and (ii) to a restaurant closing on the public holiday because of staffing costs. The third features weak Eliteness and Negativity in a quote from a local businessman that refers to him 'almost' feeling guilty for celebrating the national public holiday.

examples 42–44, words that pre-modify *day* in the nominal phrase add further confirmation of the construction of Negativity:

EX 42. . . . he said that January 26 was an "**extremely controversial day** to celebrate Australian nationhood" A17001

EX 43. . . . a local man photographed the sign "Yes, we're open on **national dickhead day**" S16049

EX 44. "It's become a kind of **discussion day** for the nation, which is good," he told The Australian. A16023

To sum up the analysis of the construction of newsworthiness in the verbal component of the AusDay corpus, it appears that in 2016/17, this public holiday was clearly associated with Negativity. Instead of falling only on the 'expected, consonant, positive side of the news values scales', that is, the 'ground' in ben-Aaron's (2003: 98–9) terms, stories published in the Australian news media relating to the Australian national day have wandered into the territory of the 'figure', in reporting on the conflict and opposition that tend to coincide with this particular day in the Australian context (as well as other types of Negativity). However, quite a different picture emerges in the construal of newsworthiness in the visual component of this dataset.

3.2 Visual DNVA of the AusDay Corpus

The 158 photographs associated with the verbal stories collected in the AusDay corpus were also analysed for the construction of newsworthiness. This analysis was collated in a MS Excel spreadsheet, noting the different news values constructed in each photograph. The general (collated) results of this analysis are shown in Figure 3.10 (in percentages).

In contrast to the verbal text, the standout news value constructed in the photographs is Positivity (68 per cent). This is followed by Eliteness (47 per cent), Proximity (32 per cent) and Personalisation (25 per cent). Positivity is largely constructed through positive facial affect (i.e. smiling faces). Since 75 per cent of all of the photographs are portrait shots, showing either one person or a pair posing for the camera, it is not surprising that this is the most dominant news value. When people **pose** for a photograph, they tend to have a positive, or at least a neutral, facial expression. Further, the portrait photography in the AusDay corpus is largely associated with stories about the Australia Day Honours. These honours figure among the highest awards that both ordinary and elite Australians can receive for services to the community or to their specialist fields. The recipients are therefore, on the whole, very pleased to receive these awards, and this Positivity is reflected in the photographs that are

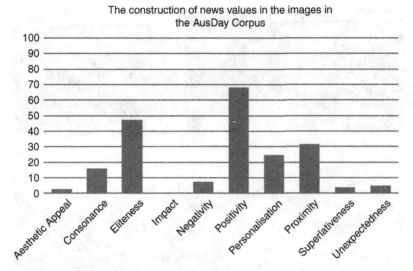

Figure 3.10 The construal of news values in the photographs in the AusDay corpus (in percentages)

published in this news storytelling. Example A in Figure 3.11 is a good example of one of these portrait shots, where a happy smiling award recipient is photographed straight on to the camera. On average, Positivity was constructed in 81 per cent of all visual reporting in *The Australian*, while it constituted 54 per cent in *The Sydney Morning Herald*.

There is only one story, published in *The Australian*, where one might detect a potential clash between the Positivity construed in the photograph and the Negativity construed in the verbal text (and other photographs with this story): the plane crash story in which two people lost their lives. This story follows news reporting convention (Bednarek & Caple, 2017: 221; Caple, 2019: 65–6), by including a (supplied) photograph of the victims, alive and smiling. The same story also includes two photographs of the plane at the point of impact, as it crashed into the river;[25] thus, the Positivity constructed in the photograph of the victims is mitigated by the Negativity constructed in the visuals of the plane crash in which they lost their lives.

---

[25] It is a relatively new phenomenon to be able to capture the moment of death (crashes, accidents, explosions), which has been facilitated by the development of smartphone technologies that include cameras and the ubiquity of surveillance cameras, along with a culture of the visual capture of our everyday lives. However, pre-digital reporting practices would still have included photographs of the aftermath of disasters/accidents along with supplied (family) photos of the victims (often smiling).

Figure 3.11 The construction of Positivity (A, C) and Negativity (B) in photographs in the AusDay corpus. PHOTOS: A: Justin McManus [S17010]; B: Justin Lloyd [A17022_6]; C: Janie Barrett [S17018_2]

Unlike in the verbal text, Negativity is constructed in only 8 per cent of the photographs in the AusDay corpus. Both newspapers report on the bad behaviour of a sporting star, Mitchell Pearce, which is captured in a still taken from a video that was posted on social media. One photograph published in *The Australian* depicts clashes between protesters and authorities at Invasion Day marches that were held throughout Australia (see Example B in Figure 3.11). However, photographs from the same event published in *The Sydney Morning Herald* show only peaceful Invasion Day protesters, as in Example C in Figure 3.11. The photographs of Invasion Day marches are the only indicators in the visual reporting of any form of opposition to the national day. One other photograph, also published by *The Sydney Morning Herald,* depicts the sign outside a café that labelled the day 'national dickhead day'. Overall, the discursive struggle that is central to the verbal news reporting of the national day is only minimally represented in the visual reporting.

Similar to the findings of the verbal analysis, the photographs in the AusDay corpus represent elites rather than ordinary individuals, with close to half of all photographs constructing Eliteness and only a quarter constructing Personalisation. Eliteness also co-occurs with Positivity (in 64 per cent of cases), and thus concurs with the findings of Bednarek and Caple (2017: 186) that politicians and other elites tend to be depicted in positive contexts as a result of their highly orchestrated public appearances. This is particularly true in relation to Australia Day events when political leaders will be ushered from one public event to the next with the press pack forming an entourage, following and reporting on these events. Bednarek and Caple (2017: 186) also note that 'ordinary citizens are more likely to be of interest to news organisations when something negative has happened to them'. Thus, one might expect Personalisation to be co-constructed with Negativity. However, in this dataset, Personalisation overwhelmingly co-occurs with Positivity (80 per cent), which reflects the nature of the event being a day of national celebration for some Australians. These photographs mostly depict very young people playing at the beach or participating in outdoor activities. The AusDay corpus also has a slight skew towards reporting about the Australia Day Honours, which, as already noted, focuses on the remarkable (positive) achievements of both ordinary and elite Australians. All of the stories about these awards include multiple photographs of award recipients, which may go some way to explaining the much higher construal of Positivity in the visuals compared with the verbal texts.

Proximity is another news value that is constructed visually in the AusDay corpus. This is achieved through the depiction of well-known/iconic Australian landmarks (the Opera House in Sydney, the Sydney Harbour Bridge, Flinders Street Station in Melbourne), or through multiple Australian flags, either worn around the shoulders of ordinary citizens or waved in the air. Consonance is also constructed in 16 per cent of photographs. Visually, Consonance is constructed through the depiction of people and their attributes that fit with the stereotypical imagery of a person/country or the staged/highly choreographed depiction of typical activities associated with a person, a group or a nation (see Section 1). A number of quite diverse impressions of Consonance emerge in the AusDay corpus. Indigenous peoples are depicted wearing traditional costumes and body paint and performing sacred ceremonies associated with important occasions (as shown in Example A in Figure 3.12). Some people are shown draped in Australian flags, with flag tattoos on their skin, and participating in activities that are typically associated with Australia Day, such as the Ute Run (Darwin), billy cart races and crab racing. The national stereotype of the barbecue (and masculinity) is depicted in a photograph of the then–Prime Minister in an apron and posing with tongs in hand in front of the barbecue. Another national

Figure 3.12 The construction of Consonance in the AusDay corpus PHOTOS: A: Kate Geraghty [S17018_1]; B: David Caird [A16015]

stereotype of multiculturalism is depicted in representations of new Australian citizens of diverse ethnic backgrounds receiving their citizenship certificates. Again, this may also signify national unity and pride in multiculturalism.

In a highly choreographed/staged photograph, an elite, Susan Alberti AC, recipient of an Australia Day Honour, is captured in front of the Australian flag, with the scarf of an Australian Rules football team draped around her neck and tossing a football (Example B in Figure 3.12). Alberti is the former Vice President of the Western Bulldogs Football Club. The photograph not only references her connection to this football club, but also establishes Consonance through a stereotypical representation of the footy-loving Australian.

Unexpectedness is constructed in eight photographs and combines most frequently with Negativity. In one instance, Unexpectedness combines with Eliteness, Personalisation and Positivity, in a photograph in which then–Prime Minister Malcolm Turnbull is captured taking a selfie with two new Australian citizens at a citizenship ceremony (see Figure 3.13). This photograph was analysed as constructing Unexpectedness, as it is usually members of the public who strive to capture a selfie with such elites, not the other way around. Again, this can also be read as a celebration of multiculturalism, presenting Australia as a non-racist land of refuge and welcome.

The fact that quite different news values are constructed in the photographs compared with the verbal text in the AusDay corpus speaks not only to the affordances of each of these semiotic modes but also to the conventions of news storytelling. Visual news storytelling, in the form of photographs, tends to focus on people, and this is certainly true of the photographs in the AusDay corpus. Only 4 of the 158 photographs do not focus on human participants. This means that either Eliteness or Personalisation are likely to be construed in many of the photographs, and since most of the photographs used in the reporting of Australia Day focus on Australia Day Honours recipients, that photography is also overwhelmingly positive.

Prime Minster Malcolm Turnbull captures a selfie of himself with newly naturalized citizens

Figure 3.13 A photograph constructing Unexpectedness, Eliteness, Personalisation and Positivity PHOTO: Andrew Meares [S16043]

3.3 Conclusion

News values in the AusDay corpus clearly reflect the discursive struggle around the national day in Australia, especially in the verbal reporting. The idea that national days can be a site of tension is not a new one. As noted in Section 1, national days, as a manifestation of 'applied nationalism', may 'have a political subtext, such as mobilising for war, promoting a policy or platform, or reconstituting the nation in minority inclusive or exclusive terms' (ben-Aaron, 2003: 77). Ben-Aaron finds, however, that news reporting on national days is mostly a 'manifestation of politeness' (2003: 97), falling on the 'expected, consonant, positive side of the news value scales' (2003: 98–9; see also ben-Aaron, 2005, Ting, 2017). However, the results from the AusDay corpus are more complex. The discursive struggle sits at the heart of the verbal reporting on Australia Day, while the visual reporting focuses on celebration and ceremony. While Negativity is constructed in the visual reporting, it is limited to depictions of the plane clash in Perth, the drunken and bad behaviour of a sporting star and clashes with police at Invasion Day rallies. Only the photographs of protesters at Invasion Day rallies hint at any discomfort or discord with respect to how Australia Day is celebrated. Viewed together, the verbal and visual reporting present the reader with a complex image of the multiple facets of this day. While some celebrate the day, others debate the day. The verbal text tends to focus on the voices of the political elite in debates around the national day, while the visuals present a more diverse picture, showing how it is not only Indigenous Australians that are calling for change, and that other Australians stand with them. Both the verbal and visual text also show some evidence of attempts to construct national unity and a sense of pride in multicultural nationhood. The next section will provide a synthesis and comparison of results from China and Australia.

4 Conclusion

We begin this section by addressing the questions we posed in Section 1 before we reflect upon the study's limitations.

4.1 Newsworthiness and National Day Reporting

As a reminder, three of our questions concerned the construction of news values:

> *What news values are discursively construed in different cultures around a similar event?*
> *How are these values typically constructed?*
> *What are the similarities and differences in what the corpus linguistic analysis uncovers and what the visual analysis uncovers?*

In sum, we found that Eliteness, Positivity, Proximity and Superlativeness are important news values in the verbal and visual construal of newsworthiness in both the Chinese and Australian corpora. Unexpectedness, Impact, and Consonance play much less of a role, and while Personalisation is an important aspect of the visual reporting, it is less so in the verbal reporting. We found limited overlap with ben-Aaron's diachronic study of national holidays in the United States (2003: 95), namely that Proximity is important, while Personalisation and Unexpectedness are less often found. Eliteness and Superlativeness seem more important in our datasets than in hers, while the low amount of Negativity in the Chinese data is similar to her findings. Overall, our study confirms the importance of Positivity in the Chinese news media (see Section 1), and we say more on Positivity in Section 4.2.

In both datasets, we also found that politicians are important in national day reporting, a point also noted by Ting (2017: 50) in relation to Malaysian reporting. However, ben-Aaron (2003: 95) states that Eliteness was only 'some-times' found in her US data, even though she points out that the national day 'is an excellent time for politicians to push forward their vision of the nation' (ben-Aaron, 2003: 92).[26] In the verbal reporting in the ChinaDay corpus, both

---

[26] Neither Ting nor ben-Aaron use the same news values approach as we do, so the comparison here is limited. For example, ben-Aaron (2003) also investigates recency, facticity, narrative conson-ance, relevance, continuity, unambiguity and attribution. Particular news values are also defined and analysed differently to DNVA. Neither study examines news values in news photography.

political and institutional elites were named using their titles/roles as they expressed their patriotism and pride in the nation. The relevant photography was highly choreographed, to the extent that the political elite and other officials were photographed in almost identical poses (and activities) year-on-year, a practice that is confirmed in more recent (2019) reporting of the national day in *Nanfang Metro* and *People's Daily* (front pages provided in Appendix 5 online, www.cambridge.org/9781108814072). In the AusDay corpus, politicians appeared to be more 'free ranging' in the types of activities they were photographed participating in; thus, the visual reporting also sometimes co-constructed Consonance and Unexpectedness.

A major difference between the two corpora relates to the construction of Negativity, which is highly important only in the Australian corpus. Here, it mostly relates to the debate around the date of the national day as expressed through the verbal reporting (see further Section 4.2). The debate per se could not be captured in all its nuance in the visual reporting, although Invasion Day marches were represented. Hence, the visual representations of citizens/non-elites demonstrated that this societal struggle is one that many Australians are participating in. Other types of Negativity relate to amoral/deviant behaviour, workplace issues and accidental death, some of which also occurs in the ChinaDay corpus (e.g. photos that show people disrespecting ancient monuments for a photo opportunity).

In relation to Australia Day, our analysis of the visual and verbal resources gives a complementary picture of what this day represents. It is a day of both celebration (mostly visually construed) and of struggle (mostly verbally construed). Analysis of only one semiotic mode (words or photographs) would have given only a partial understanding of how the national day is constructed as newsworthy. By examining these news items in their multimodal richness, as presented to audiences, the discursive struggle about the national day is revealed in all its complexity.

Likewise, our analysis of both visual and verbal resources construing the Chinese national day as newsworthy gives important insights into how these Chinese newspapers operate. The focus in the verbal reporting is very much on the positive face of the national day, as expressed through the political elites. The visual reporting, however, gives a broader view of the newsworthy aspects of the national day, some of which are negative and more concerned with non-elites (congestion, pollution, difficulties travelling during the holiday period). This variety mostly comes from the visual reporting of the *Nanfang Metro*, which is seen as providing more informative reporting than the national newspapers, such as *People's Daily* (see Section 1). Another important insight from this study points to the level of control exerted over what is reported and how it is reported, resulting in the similar construal of news values in both newspapers across both years. A vital next step for this research would be to investigate how and where this control is enacted: through self-regulation at the point of news gathering, through editorial decisions or through other external factors.

A final, important point is the need to independently develop inventories of linguistic resources for constructing newsworthiness in a particular language. In our case, we took the news values as the departure point, and Changpeng Huan established whether and how these values are constructed in the Chinese data. However, it is clear that more research is necessary on the construction of news values in Chinese. In this Element we have focused more on the results of the analysis than on the resources per se (see further Section 4.3).

4.2 Newsworthiness and National Identity

Another question we asked in Section 1 was: *How does the construction of newsworthiness relate to national identity?* We assume here, following Anderson (1991: 4), that nationality is a cultural artefact. According to Anderson, the nation can be defined as 'an imagined political community – and imagined as both inherently limited and sovereign' (Anderson, 1991: 6). Wodak et al. (2009) argue that this 'imaginary community' is 'constructed and conveyed in discourse, predominantly in narratives of national culture' (2009: 22). Similarly, Hall sees nations as symbolic communities, and national cultures as discourses, and suggests that the discursive construction of national identity is contained in the stories, memories and images that we share about 'nation' (Hall, 1996: 613). While there are many ways in which national identity is discursively constructed (e.g. Billig, 1995, on 'banal nationalism'), media coverage of the national day is clearly relevant. National days are a celebration of nationhood, and a time for remembering the past. They belong to the 'national identity projects' that allow members of a nation to 'reconcile the distinct features of the different regions and ethnic groups that constitute a nation' (Stanojević & Šarić, 2019: 6). National days feature the singing of national anthems, which Anderson (1991) calls 'the echoed physical realization of the imagined community', and citizenship ceremonies held on national days in Australia showcase those '"invited into" the imagined community' through naturalisation (1991: 145). In turn, national day media coverage has been regarded as important for reinforcing hegemony and promoting national identity and patriotism (ben-Aaron, 2003: 98; Ting, 2017: 53).

Our entry point into the data was news values rather than national identity (or other types of values), but this analysis does inform us about the discursive construction of national identity. This is especially the case when we examine Positivity. In the Australian data, Positivity is mostly construed in the visual reporting. This is because much of the Australia Day reporting focuses on the Australia Day Honours, featuring many photographs of the smiling recipients. These awards celebrate the outstanding contributions of both ordinary and elite Australians and construct an image of Australia as a nation where its citizens selflessly support each other. In the verbal reporting, Positivity is occasionally constructed in relation to multiculturalism and reconciliation.

In the Chinese data, Positivity is constructed in relation to valued behaviours (e.g. participating in national day ceremonies or volunteering during the holidays) and reflect key Chinese values such as 礼/rites, 和/harmony and 爱国/patriotism (Shi-xu, 2014: 61). References to the SARs Macau and Hong Kong also give a sense of 'cultural unity in diversity' (Shi-xu, 2014: 62). For historical reasons, the promotion of patriotism and the valorisation of nationalism are important in Chinese discourse today, and have been interpreted as arising from the experience of colonialism (Shi-xu, 2014: 98–101; cf. Gao, 2018). The overwhelming Positivity in the ChinaDay corpus might be interpreted from a Western perspective as 'propaganda', but this could equally be regarded as 宣传, defined as 'public communication (i.e. informing, educating and mobilizing the public, often through mass media) for the politics of societal stability and development' (Shi-xu, 2014: 70). Moreover, the analysis of the Chinese news reporting resembles ben-Aaron's analysis of US reporting:

> As a whole, the news coverage valorizes having proper feelings, and displaying them through local socially appropriate reactions to events, occasions, and ritually charged objects – all seen in terms of exhibiting proper citizen behavior. (ben-Aaron, 2005: 712)

Aspects of both Australian and Chinese coverage are also reminiscent of the value of 'unity in ethnic diversity' mentioned in Ting (2017) in the Malaysian context.

In addition to Positivity, Negativity – in the Australian coverage – also informs us about national identity. While other types of Negativity are present, in general this Negativity (re-)produces the discursive struggle in contemporary Australian society between different narratives of the nation. When activists ask to 'change the date', they recognise that '[n]ations ... have no clearly identifiable births' (Anderson, 1991: 205). By labelling 26 January *Invasion Day*, they construct a different narrative of the nation than when it is called *Australia Day*. When newspapers report on this conflict, they do **not** construct the nation as a harmonious community, rather showing that not everyone wants to participate in or can identify with a hegemonic idea of the nation where its birth is linked to colonialism.

This discursive construction is also influenced by the 'material' reality, that is, increasing support for protest/activist movements and the campaign to 'change the date' (see Section 1). This is arguably a sign of healthy news reporting in a functioning democracy with a free press. An alternative, more nationalistic, approach would be for newspapers to ignore such criticism and protests and only focus on the positive aspects of the day. In the US context, ben-Aaron found that – with the exception of the Vietnam War protests – Negativity is 'usually absent from stories about national holidays' (ben-Aaron, 2003: 95). She states that 'protests and controversy are rarely foregrounded in same-day and next-day coverage, but are discussed at a safe remove, either before or after the holiday period, or in smaller stories "buried" in the newspaper' (2003: 88). It must be noted here that results for the United States could be different if we examined reporting about contested days, such as Columbus Day, commemorating when Christopher Columbus arrived in the Americas in October 1492. Several US states and cities no longer celebrate Columbus Day, with some instead celebrating Indigenous Peoples Day (Yan, 2018). In other words, it is apparent that differences in reporting also depend on the nature of the event that is being celebrated in each country.

It is also clear that if there are no protests then newspapers cannot report on such. We collected the Chinese data in 2015 and 2016, when there were no protests to our knowledge (in contrast to Australia). In that respect, it is interesting to briefly turn to 2019, when protests (against an extradition bill introduced in April 2019 – not related to the national day) were ongoing in Hong Kong including on the national day (1 October), when an eighteen-year-old protester was shot in the chest with a live bullet (BBC News, 2019). Changpeng Huan scanned both *Nanfang Metro* and *People's Daily* on 2 October 2019, and found no mention of the protests or the shooting in Hong Kong. Only *People's Daily* briefly mentioned (on page 4) Hong Kong and Macau raising the national flag to celebrate the national day.

As mentioned, our starting point was the analysis of news values. An alternative analysis would have foregrounded the analysis of national identity, but perhaps at the expense of ignoring news values. We did relate news values to concepts such as discursive struggle and national identity, but this does not provide a full picture: for instance, we did not focus on evaluation/stance/ appraisal or audience positioning (how newspapers position their audiences and affiliate with them). Clearly, protests can be evaluated differently by the newspapers, which can adopt a negative, neutral or positive stance towards them, most likely in line with their political leaning. We would therefore predict that such an analysis would uncover a negative stance in *The Australian* (right-leaning) and a positive or neutral stance in *The Sydney Morning Herald* (left-leaning). Another example is that the use of flags can be tied to the promotion of patriotism and rallying of the populace under one national identity (Ting, 2017), whereas a news values approach links this to Proximity. In other words, a news values lens provides a different perspective on the data, even if findings can then be linked to other types of analysis.

4.3 Methodological Reflections

There are several limitations to our approach to the cross-linguistic corpus-assisted multimodal discourse analysis of newsworthiness: Although we analysed all of the photographs published with each story, we only analysed news values established in the immediate co-text of references to the national day. In other words, we did not analyse complete texts. There are two reasons for this approach: First, we wanted to use techniques that can also be used for much larger datasets. In Potts et al. (2015), for example, we applied similar techniques to analyse news values in a 36-million-word corpus. While analysis of full texts would have been possible for our small dataset, it is difficult to scale this up to bigger corpora. Secondly, the complexity of our approach and of the data we analysed also constrained us – not only did we analyse both language and photographs, we also analysed data from two different languages and four different newspapers. Another limitation is that we only used a small number of corpus linguistic techniques (word frequency, collocation, concordance). Taking a different starting point, such as keywords of the two corpora (Baker & Vessey, 2018), might have produced different results. Further reflections on the corpus linguistic aspects of our approach can be found in Bednarek et al. in press and an example analysis of a complete text is available at www.newsvaluesanalysis.com (under 'our book' > 'extensions').

In addition, our approach to the analysis of the Chinese media was largely 'Western-centric' (for criticism, see Shi-xu, 2014), and we assumed that the previously identified news values are at play in the Chinese news context. Cross-linguistic corpus analysis comes with its own challenges (see Section 1 and the relevant discussions in Vessey, 2013, Taylor, 2014). While our approach did not require the identification of (near) translation equivalents, it did require a framework for analysing how news values are constructed in each language. We attempted to solve this issue by **not** simply applying the English-language framework but rather taking the news values as starting points and inductively identifying how these are constructed in Chinese. However, much more research on a wider set of data and topics is necessary to develop a comprehensive Chinese-language framework that could be used by other researchers. Furthermore, it is necessary to interrogate further whether the assumed news values are relevant to the contemporary China media landscape (see Section 1). An additional challenge we faced was that it was difficult to discuss the concordance analysis of the Chinese data among all authors, given that two of us did not have any knowledge of the language. This made it harder to reach a consensus about the concordance analysis, and we had to rely on the translations to do so.

The general limitations of DNVA are outlined in Bednarek and Caple (2017: 44–5); thus we do not rehearse those here. However, we also note the necessary focus of DNVA on news reporting, as opposed to other text types such as editorials, user comments or social media posts, which can be used to express opinion and for activism (see Caple & Bednarek, in press, on #invasionday on Instagram).

4.4 Concluding Remarks

Our study demonstrates the context-dependence of newsworthiness construction even in relation to shared events such as national days. What we find for a particular newspaper in relation to a particular country's national day cannot be predicted to hold for other newspapers and other countries or even other public holidays (e.g. Independence vs Columbus Day in the United States). Differences between countries not only depend on their political system and the extent of press freedom/censorship, but also on the strength of nationalism as a cultural value and the particular historical event that is marked by the national day. Ultimately, the construction of newsworthiness is influenced by multiple factors, while DNVA provides discourse analysts with a robust framework for analysing how it is constructed through both verbal and visual resources.

References

Anderson, B. (1991). *Imagined Communities: Reflections on the Origin and Spread of Nationalism*, revised and extended edition. London: Verso.

Anthony, L. (2016) *AntConc* (Version 3.4.2) [Computer Software]. Tokyo, Japan: Waseda University. www.laurenceanthony.net/software

AIATSIS (Australian Institute of Aboriginal and Torres Strait Islander Studies) (2018). Day of Mourning – 26th January 1938. Date viewed: 31/01/2020. https://aiatsis.gov.au/exhibitions/day-mourning-26th-january-1938

Australia Day Council (2018). About Australia Day: History [Australia Day timeline compiled by Dr Elizabeth Kwan]. Date viewed: 30/08/2019. www.australiaday.org.au/about-australia-day/history/

Baker, P. (2012). Acceptable bias? Using corpus linguistics methods with Critical Discourse Analysis. *Critical Discourse Studies*, 9(3), 247–56.

Baker, P., & Egbert, J. (eds.) (2016). *Triangulating Methodological Approaches in Corpus-Linguistic Research*. London: Routledge.

Baker, P., Gabrielatos, C., Khosravinik, M., Krzyzanowski, M., McEnery, T., & Wodak, R. (2008). A useful methodological synergy? Combining critical discourse analysis and corpus linguistics to examine discourses of refugees and asylum seekers in the UK press. *Discourse & Society*, 19 (3), 273–306.

Baker, P., Gabrielatos, C., & McEnery, T. (2013). *Discourse Analysis and Media Attitudes: The Representation of Islam in the British Press*. Cambridge: Cambridge Univeristy Press.

Baker, P., & Vessey, R. (2018). A corpus-driven comparison of English and French Islamist extremist texts. *International Journal of Corpus Linguistics*, 23(3), 255–78.

BBC News (2019). China anniversary: Hong Kong protester shot by live round (1 October 2019). www.bbc.com/news/world-asia-china–49891403

Bednarek, M. (2006). *Evaluation in Media Discourse: Analysis of a Newspaper Corpus*. London/New York: Continuum.

Bednarek, M. (2008). Semantic preference and semantic prosody re-examined. *Corpus Linguistics and Linguistic Theory*, 4(2), 119–139.

Bednarek, M. (2016a). Voices and values in the news: News media talk, news values and attribution. *Discourse, Context & Media*, 11, 27–37.

Bednarek, M. (2016b). Coding manual for the analysis of news values using UAM Corpus Tool. www.newsvaluesanalysis.com

Bednarek, M., & Caple, H. (2012). *News Discourse*. London/New York: Continuum.

Bednarek, M., & Caple, H. (2014). Why do news values matter? Towards a new methodological framework for analyzing news discourse in Critical Discourse Analysis and beyond. *Discourse & Society*, 25(2), 135–58.

Bednarek, M., & Caple, H. (2017). *The Discourse of News Values: How News Organizations Create Newsworthiness*. New York: Oxford University Press.

Bednarek, M., Caple, H., & Huan, C. (in press). Computer-based analysis of news values: A case study on national day reporting. *Journalism Studies*.

Bell, A. (1991). *The Language of News Media*. Oxford: Blackwell.

Belsey, C. (1984). The politics of meaning. In F. Barker, P. Hulme, M. Iversen & D. Loxley, eds., *Confronting the Crisis: War, Politics and Culture in the Eighties. The Proceedings of the Essex Sociology of Literature Conference, July 1983*. Colchester: University of Essex, pp.27–38.

ben-Aaron, D. (2003). When news isn't news: The case of national holidays. *Journal of Historical Pragmatics*, 4(1), 75–102.

ben-Aaron, D. (2005). Given and news: Evaluation in newspaper stories about national anniversaries. *Text*, 25(5), 691–718.

Billig, M. (1995). *Banal Nationalism*. London: Sage.

Brezina, V., McEnery, T., & Wattam, S. (2015). Collocations in context: A new perspective on collocation networks. *International Journal of Corpus Linguistics*, 20(2), 139–73.

Caple, H. (2013). *Photojournalism: A Social Semiotic Approach*. Basingstoke: Palgrave Macmillan.

Caple, H. (2018a). Analysing the multimodal text. In C. Taylor & A. Marchi, eds., *Corpus Approaches to Discourse*. London/New York: Routledge, pp.85–109.

Caple, H. (2018b). News values and newsworthiness. In H. Ornebring, ed., *Oxford Research Encyclopedia of Communication*. Oxford: Oxford University Press, pp. 1–21.

Caple, H. (2019). *Photojournalism Disrupted: The View from Australia*. Abingdon: Routledge.

Caple, H., & Bednarek, M. (in press). A nation remembers: Discourses of change, mourning, and reconciliation on Australia Day. In M. Zappavigna & S. Dreyfus, eds., *Discourses of Hope and Reconciliation. On J. R. Martin's Contribution to Systemic Functional Linguistics*. London: Bloomsbury.

Carpentier, N. (2018). Discourse-theoretical analysis. In J. Flowerdew & J. E. Richardson, eds., *The Routledge Handbook of Critical Discourse Studies*. Abingdon: Routledge, pp. 359–75.

Chan, J. M. (2019). From networked commercialism to networked authoritarianism: The biggest challenge to journalism. *Journalism*, 20(1), 64–8.

Clure, E. (2017). City of Yarra council's 'attack on Australia Day' angers Malcolm Turnbull. *ABC News*, 16 August. Date viewed: 18/10/17. www.abc.net.au/news/2017–08-15/melbourne-council-votes-to-ban-references-to-australia-day/8810286

Cotter, C. (2010). *News Talk: Investigating the Language of Journalism*. Cambridge: Cambridge University Press.

Daille, B. (1995). Combined Approach for Terminology Extraction: Lexical Statistics and Linguistic Filtering. *UCREL Technical Papers*, No. 15, Department of Linguistics, Lancaster University, Lancaster, UK.

Djonov, E., & Zhao, S. (eds.) (2014). *Critical Multimodal Studies of Popular Culture*. London/New York: Routledge.

Eades, D. (2006). Lexical struggle in court: Aboriginal Australians versus the state. *Journal of Sociolinguistics*, 10(2), 153–180.

Fairclough, N. (1995). *Media Discourse*. London: Bloomsbury.

Fruttaldo, A., & Venuti, M. (2017). A cross-cultural discursive approach to news values in the press in the US, the UK and Italy: The case of the Supreme Court ruling on same-sex marriage. *ESP Across Cultures*, 14, 81–97.

Gang, Q., & Bandurski, D. (2011). China's emerging public sphere: The impact of media commercialization, professionalism, and the Internet in an era of transition. In S. L. Shirk, ed., *Changing Media, Changing China*. Oxford: Oxford University Press, pp. 38–76.

Gao, M. (2018). *Constructing China: Clashing Views of the People's Republic*. London: Pluto Press.

Grundmann, R., & Krishnamurthy, R. (2010). The discourse of climate change: A corpus-based approach. *Critical Approaches to Discourse Analysis across Disciplines*, 4(2), 125–46.

Hall, S. (1996). The question of cultural identity. In S. Hall, D. Held, D. Hubert & K. Thompson, eds., *Modernity: An Introduction to Modern Societies*. Oxford: Wiley, pp. 595–634.

Huan, C. (2016). Leaders or readers, whom to please? News values in the transition of the Chinese press. *Discourse, Context & Media*, 13, 114–21.

Huan, C. (2018). *Journalistic Stance in Chinese and Australian Hard News*. Singapore: Springer.

Jaworska, S., & Krishnamurty, R. (2012). On the F-word: A corpus-based analysis of the media representation of feminism in British and German press discourse, 1990–2009. *Discourse & Society*, 23(4), 401–31.

Jin, G., Xiao, H., Fu, L., & Zhang, Y. (2005). The construction and deep processing of Modern Chinese Corpus [现代汉语语料库建设及深加工]. *Applied Linguistics* [语言文字应用], 2, 111–20.

Jørgensen, M., & Phillips, L.J. (2002). *Discourse Analysis as Theory and Method*. London: Sage.

Laclau, E., & Mouffe, C. (1985). *Hegemony and Socialist Strategy: Towards a Radical Democratic Politics*. London: Verso.

Louw, B. (1993). Irony in the text or insincerity in the writer? In M. Baker, G. Francis & E. Tognini-Bonelli, eds., *Text and Technology: In Honour of John Sinclair*. Amsterdam/Philadelphia: John Benjamins, pp. 157–76.

Machin, D. (2013). What is multimodal critical discourse studies? *Critical Discourse Studies*, 10(4), 347–55.

Machin, D., & Mayr, A. (2012). *How to Do Critical Discourse Analysis: A Multimodal Introduction*. London: Sage.

Marchi, A., & Taylor, C. (2009). If on a winter's night two researchers …: A challenge to assumptions of soundness of interpretation. *Critical Approaches to Discourse Analysis across Disciplines CADAAD Journal*, 3 (1), 1–20.

Mautner, G. (2000). *Der britische Europa-Diskurs. Methodenreflexion und Fallstudien zur Berichterstattung in der Tagespresse*. [The British Discourse on Europe. Methodological Observations and Case Studies on Daily Press Reportage]. Wien: Passagen Verlag.

Nartey, M., & Mwinlaaru, I.N. (2019). Towards a decade of synergising corpus linguistics and critical discourse analysis: a meta-analysis. *Corpora*, 14(2), 203–35.

Nation, I. S. P., & Waring, R. (1997). Vocabulary size, text coverage, and word lists. In N. Schmitt & M. McCarthy, eds., *Vocabulary: Description, Acquisition and Pedagogy*. Cambridge: Cambridge University Press, pp. 6–19.

NITV (2017). Australia Day, Invasion Day, Survival Day: What's in a name? Date viewed: 31/01/20. www.sbs.com.au/nitv/explainer/australia-day-invasion-day-survival-day-whats-name

Partington, A., Duguid, A., & Taylor, C. (2013). *Patterns and Meanings in Discourse: Theory and Practice in Corpus-Assisted Discourse Studies (CADS)*. Amsterdam: John Benjamins.

Potts, A., Bednarek, M., & Caple, H. (2015). How can computer-based methods help researchers to investigate news values in large datasets? A corpus linguistic study of the construction of newsworthiness in the reporting on Hurricane Katrina. *Discourse & Communication*, 9(2): 149–172.

Public Holidays Global (2019). National Day 2019 and 2020. Date viewed: 20/ 08/19. https://publicholidays.cn/national-day/

Scott, M. (2017–19). *WordSmith Tools* (Version 7) [Computer Software]. Stroud: Lexical Analysis Software.

Shi-xu (2014). *Chinese Discourse Studies*. Basingstoke: Palgrave Macmillan.

Shirk, S. L. (ed.) (2011). *Changing Media, Changing China*. Oxford: Oxford University Press.

Sinclair, J. (2005). Corpus and text: Basic principles. In M. Wynne, ed., *Developing Linguistic Corpora: A Guide to Good Practice*. Oxford: Oxbow, pp.1–16.

Stanojević, M-M. & Šarić, L. (2019). Metaphors in the discursive construction of nations. In L. Šarić & M-M. Stanojević. eds., *Metaphor, Nation and Discourse*. Amsterdam: John Benjamins, pp. 1–34.

Sun, W. (2012). Rescaling media in China: The formations of local, provincial, and regional media cultures. *Chinese Journal of Communication*, 5(1), 10–15.

Taylor, C. (2014). Investigating the representation of migrants in the UK and Italian press: A cross-linguistic corpus-assisted discourse analysis. *International Journal of Corpus Linguistics*, 19(3), 368–400.

Ting, S. H. (2017). An agenda-setting study of national day coverage in state and national newspapers. *3L: The Southeast Asian Journal of English Language Studies*, 23(4), 41–55.

Trindall, S. (2019). Every day is Survival Day in the colony of Australia. *Guardian Australia, Indigenous X*, 24 January. Date viewed: 21/01/20. www.theguardian.com/commentisfree/2019/jan/24/every-day-is-survival-day-in-the-colony-of-australia?

University of Sydney (2018). Ask us anything: Aboriginal and Torres Strait Islander people. Date viewed: 31/01/20. www.youtube.com/watch? v=SHVbVBLlhCM

van Dijk, T. A. (1998). *Ideology. A Multidisciplinary Approach*. London: Sage.

Vessey, R. (2013). Challenges in cross-linguistic corpus-assisted discourse studies. *Corpora*, 8(1), 1–26.

Walhquist, C. (2017). Second Melbourne council votes to cancel Australia Day ceremony and celebrations. *Guardian Australia*, 21 August. Date viewed: 18/ 10/17. www.theguardian.com/australia-news/2017/aug/21/second-melbourne-council-votes-to-cancel-australia-day-ceremony-and-celebrations

Wodak, R., de Cillia, R. Reisigl, M., & Liebhart, K. (2009). *The Discursive Construction of National Identity*, Second Edition. Edinburgh: Edinburgh University Press.

Wu, C. (2009). Corpus-based research. In M. A. K. Halliday & J. Webster, eds., *Continuum Companion to Systemic Functional Linguistics*. London: Continuum, pp. 128–42.

Wu, D. D., & Ng, P. (2011). Becoming global, remaining local: The discourses of international news reporting by CCTV-4 and Phoenix TV Hong Kong. *Critical Arts: South-North Cultural and Media Studies*, 25(1), 73–87.

Xiao, R., & McEnery, T. (2006). Collocation, semantic prosody, and near synonymy: A cross-linguistic perspective. *Applied Linguistics*, 27(1), 103–29.

Yan, H. (2018). Across the US, more cities ditch Columbus Day to honor those who really discovered America. *CNN*, 8 October. Date viewed: 14/11/19. https://edition.cnn.com/2018/10/08/us/columbus-day-vs-indigenous-peoples-day/index.html

Acknowledgements

This project was partially funded by The National Social Science Fund of China from the National Office for Philosophy and Social Sciences (grant no. 19CYY016) and an Australian Research Council DECRA [Project ID: DE160100120]. The views expressed herein are those of the authors and are not necessarily those of the Australian Government or Australian Research Council.

We are immensely grateful to colleagues in Australia and China who participated in workshops on DNVA and who read and commented on chapter drafts. In particular, we would like to thank Ping Tian, Jun Li and attendees of the DNVA workshop at the Halliday-Hasan International Lectures & the 3rd GDUFS Multiliteracies Forum, Guangdong Foreign Studies University, Guangzhou, China, 2018.

A few sections of this Element incorporate partial content from earlier research on DNVA or Australia Day, which appears respectively in Bednarek, M. and Caple, H. (2017) *The Discourse of News Values. How News Organizations Create Newsworthiness*. Oxford: Oxford University Press; Caple, H. and Bednarek, M. (in press). A nation remembers: Discourses of change, mourning, and reconciliation on Australia Day. In M. Zappavigna & S. Dreyfus, eds., *Discourses of Hope and Reconciliation. On J. R. Martin's Contribution to Systemic Functional Linguistics*. London: Bloomsbury; and Bednarek, M., Caple, H. and Huan, C. (in press). Computer-based analysis of news values: A case study on national day reporting. *Journalism Studies*, copyright Taylor & Francis, available online: http://www.tandfonline.com/10.1080/1461670X.2020.1807393.

Cambridge Elements ≡

Corpus Linguistics

Susan Hunston
University of Birmingham
Professor of English Language at the University of Birmingham, UK. She has been involved in Corpus Linguistics for many years and has written extensively on corpora, discourse, and the lexis-grammar interface. She is probably best known as the author of *Corpora in Applied Linguistics* (2002, Cambridge University Press). Susan is currently co-editor, with Carol Chapelle, of the Cambridge Applied Linguistics series.

Advisory Board

About the Series
Corpus Linguistics has grown to become part of the mainstream of Linguistics and Applied Linguistics, as well as being used as an adjunct to other forms of discourse analysis in a variety of fields. It continues to become increasingly complex, both in terms of the methods it uses and in relation to the theoretical concepts it engages with. The Cambridge Elements in Corpus Linguistics series has been designed to meet the needs of both students and researchers who need to keep up with this changing field. The series includes introductions to the main topic areas by experts in the field as well as accounts of the latest ideas and developments by leading researchers.

Cambridge Elements ≡

Corpus Linguistics

Elements in the Series

Multimodal News Analysis across Cultures
Helen Caple, Changpeng Huan and Monika Bednarek

A full series listing is available at: www.cambridge.org/corpuslinguistics

Printed in the United States
By Bookmasters